MODERN WORLD LEADERS

# Hugo Chávez

# MODERN WORLD LEADERS

## MODERN WORLD LEADERS

# Hugo Chávez

Judith Levin

**CHELSEA HOUSE**
**P U B L I S H E R S**
An imprint of Infobase Publishing

**Hugo Chávez**

Chelsea House
An imprint of Infobase Publishing
132 West 31st Street
New York, NY 10001

**Library of Congress Cataloging-in-Publication Data**

Levin, Judith, 1956–
  Hugo Chávez / Judith Levin.
    p. cm. — (Modern world leaders)
  Includes bibliographical references and index.
  ISBN 0-7910-9258-5 (hardcover)
  1. Chávez Frías, Hugo—Juvenile literature. 2. Venezuela—Politics and government—1974–1999—Juvenile literature. 3. Venezuela—Politics and government—1999—Juvenile literature 4. Presidents—Venezuela—Biography—Juvenile literature.  I. Title. II. Series.
  F2328.52.C48L48 2006
  987.06'42092—dc22              2006010611

Chelsea House books are available at special discounts when purchased in bulk quantities for businesses, associations, institutions, or sales promotions. Please call our Special Sales Department in New York at (212) 967-8800 or (800) 322-8755.

You can find Chelsea House on the World Wide Web at http://www.chelseahouse.com

Text design by Erik Lindstrom
Cover design by Takeshi Takahashi

Printed in the United States of America

Bang FOF 10 9 8 7 6 5 4 3 2 1

This book is printed on acid-free paper.

All links and Web addresses were checked and verified to be correct at the time of publication. Because of the dynamic nature of the Web, some addresses and links may have changed since publication and may no longer be valid.

# TABLE OF CONTENTS

ARTHUR M. SCHLESINGER, JR.

# On Leadership

L eadership, it may be said, is really what makes the world go round. Love no doubt smoothes the passage; but love is a private transaction between consenting adults. Leadership is a public transaction with history. The idea of leadership affirms the capacity of individuals to move, inspire, and mobilize masses of people so that they act together in pursuit of an end. Sometimes leadership serves good purposes, sometimes bad; but whether the end is benign or evil, great leaders are those men and women who leave their personal stamp on history.

Now, the very concept of leadership implies the proposition that individuals can make a difference. This proposition has never been universally accepted. From classical times to the present day, eminent thinkers have regarded individuals as no more than the agents and pawns of larger forces, whether the gods and goddesses of the ancient world or, in the modern era, race, class, nation, the dialectic, the will of the people, the spirit of the times, history itself. Against such forces, the individual dwindles into insignificance.

So contends the thesis of historical determinism. Tolstoy's great novel *War and Peace* offers a famous statement of the case. Why, Tolstoy asked, did millions of men in the Napoleonic Wars, denying their human feelings and their common sense, move back and forth across Europe slaughtering their fellows? "The war," Tolstoy answered, "was bound to happen simply because it was bound to happen." All prior history determined it. As for leaders, they, Tolstoy said, "are but the labels that serve to give a name to an end and, like labels, they have the least possible connection with the event." The greater the leader, "the more conspicuous the inevitability and the predestination of every act he commits." The leader, said Tolstoy, is "the slave of history."

Determinism takes many forms. Marxism is the determinism of class. Nazism the determinism of race. But the idea of men and women as the slaves of history runs athwart the deepest human instincts. Rigid determinism abolishes the idea of human freedom—the assumption of free choice that underlies every move we make, every word we speak, every thought we think. It abolishes the idea of human responsibility, since it is manifestly unfair to reward or punish people for actions that are by definition beyond their control. No one can live consistently by any deterministic creed. The Marxist states prove this themselves by their extreme susceptibility to the cult of leadership.

More than that, history refutes the idea that individuals make no difference. In December 1931, a British politician crossing Fifth Avenue in New York City between 76th and 77th streets around 10:30 P.M. looked in the wrong direction and was knocked down by an automobile—a moment, he later recalled, of a man aghast, a world aglare: "I do not understand why I was not broken like an eggshell or squashed like a gooseberry." Fourteen months later an American politician, sitting in an open car in Miami, Florida, was fired on by an assassin; the man beside him was hit. Those who believe that individuals make no difference to history might well ponder whether the next two decades would have been the same had Mario Constasino's car killed Winston Churchill in 1931 and Giuseppe Zangara's bullet killed Franklin Roosevelt in 1933. Suppose, in addition, that Lenin had died of typhus in Siberia in 1895 and that Hitler had been killed on the western front in 1916. What would the twentieth century have looked like now?

For better or for worse, individuals do make a difference. "The notion that a people can run itself and its affairs anonymously," wrote the philosopher William James, "is now well known to be the silliest of absurdities. Mankind does nothing save through initiatives on the part of inventors, great or small, and imitation by the rest of us—these are the sole factors in human progress. Individuals of genius show the way, and set the patterns, which common people then adopt and follow."

Leadership, James suggests, means leadership in thought as well as in action. In the long run, leaders in thought may well make the greater difference to the world. "The ideas of economists and political philosophers, both when they are right and when they are wrong," wrote John Maynard Keynes, "are more powerful than is commonly understood. Indeed the world is ruled by little else. Practical men, who believe themselves to be quite exempt from any intellectual influences, are usually the slaves of some defunct economist. . . . The power of vested interests is vastly exaggerated compared with the gradual encroachment of ideas."

But, as Woodrow Wilson once said, "Those only are leaders of men, in the general eye, who lead in action. . . . It is at their hands that new thought gets its translation into the crude language of deeds." Leaders in thought often invent in solitude and obscurity, leaving to later generations the tasks of imitation. Leaders in action—the leaders portrayed in this series—have to be effective in their own time.

And they cannot be effective by themselves. They must act in response to the rhythms of their age. Their genius must be adapted, in a phrase from William James, "to the receptivities of the moment." Leaders are useless without followers. "There goes the mob," said the French politician, hearing a clamor in the streets. "I am their leader. I must follow them." Great leaders turn the inchoate emotions of the mob to purposes of their own. They seize on the opportunities of their time, the hopes, fears, frustrations, crises, potentialities. They succeed when events have prepared the way for them, when the community is awaiting to be aroused, when they can provide the clarifying and organizing ideas. Leadership completes the circuit between the individual and the mass and thereby alters history.

It may alter history for better or for worse. Leaders have been responsible for the most extravagant follies and most monstrous crimes that have beset suffering humanity. They have also been vital in such gains as humanity has made in individual freedom, religious and racial tolerance, social justice, and respect for human rights.

There is no sure way to tell in advance who is going to lead for good and who for evil. But a glance at the gallery of men and women in MODERN WORLD LEADERS suggests some useful tests.

One test is this: Do leaders lead by force or by persuasion? By command or by consent? Through most of history leadership was exercised by the divine right of authority. The duty of followers was to defer and to obey. "Theirs not to reason why/Theirs but to do and die." On occasion, as with the so-called enlightened despots of the eighteenth century in Europe, absolutist leadership was animated by humane purposes. More often, absolutism nourished the passion for domination, land, gold, and conquest and resulted in tyranny.

The great revolution of modern times has been the revolution of equality. "Perhaps no form of government," wrote the British historian James Bryce in his study of the United States, *The American Commonwealth*, "needs great leaders so much as democracy." The idea that all people should be equal in their legal condition has undermined the old structure of authority, hierarchy, and deference. The revolution of equality has had two contrary effects on the nature of leadership. For equality, as Alexis de Tocqueville pointed out in his great study *Democracy in America*, might mean equality in servitude as well as equality in freedom.

"I know of only two methods of establishing equality in the political world," Tocqueville wrote. "Rights must be given to every citizen, or none at all to anyone . . . save one, who is the master of all." There was no middle ground "between the sovereignty of all and the absolute power of one man." In his astonishing prediction of twentieth-century totalitarian dictatorship, Tocqueville explained how the revolution of equality could lead to the *Führerprinzip* and more terrible absolutism than the world had ever known.

But when rights are given to every citizen and the sovereignty of all is established, the problem of leadership takes a new form, becomes more exacting than ever before. It is easy to issue commands and enforce them by the rope and the stake, the concentration camp and the *gulag*. It is much harder to use argument and achievement to overcome opposition and win consent. The Founding Fathers of the United States understood the difficulty. They believed that history had given them the opportunity to decide, as Alexander Hamilton wrote in the first Federalist Paper, whether men are indeed capable of basing government on "reflection and choice, or whether they are forever destined to depend . . . on accident and force."

Government by reflection and choice called for a new style of leadership and a new quality of followership. It required leaders to be responsive to popular concerns, and it required followers to be active and informed participants in the process. Democracy does not eliminate emotion from politics; sometimes it fosters demagoguery; but it is confident that, as the greatest of democratic leaders put it, you cannot fool all of the people all of the time. It measures leadership by results and retires those who overreach or falter or fail.

It is true that in the long run despots are measured by results too. But they can postpone the day of judgment, sometimes indefinitely, and in the meantime they can do infinite harm. It is also true that democracy is no guarantee of virtue and intelligence in government, for the voice of the people is not necessarily the voice of God. But democracy, by assuring the right of opposition, offers built-in resistance to the evils inherent in absolutism. As the theologian Reinhold Niebuhr summed it up, "Man's capacity for justice makes democracy possible, but man's inclination to justice makes democracy necessary."

A second test for leadership is the end for which power is sought. When leaders have as their goal the supremacy of a master race or the promotion of totalitarian revolution or the acquisition and exploitation of colonies or the protection of greed and privilege or the preservation of personal power, it is likely that their leadership will do little to advance the cause of humanity. When their goal is the abolition of slavery, the liberation of women, the enlargement of opportunity for the poor and powerless, the extension of equal rights to racial minorities, the defense of the freedoms of expression and opposition, it is likely that their leadership will increase the sum of human liberty and welfare.

Leaders have done great harm to the world. They have also conferred great benefits. You will find both sorts in this series. Even "good" leaders must be regarded with a certain wariness. Leaders are not demigods; they put on their trousers one leg after another just like ordinary mortals. No leader is infallible, and every leader needs to be reminded of this at regular intervals. Irreverence irritates leaders but is their salvation. Unquestioning submission corrupts leaders and demeans followers. Making a cult of a leader is always a mistake. Fortunately hero worship generates its own antidote. "Every hero," said Emerson, "becomes a bore at last."

The single benefit the great leaders confer is to embolden the rest of us to live according to our own best selves, to be active, insistent, and resolute in affirming our own sense of things. For great leaders attest to the reality of human freedom against the supposed inevitabilities of history. And they attest to the wisdom and power that may lie within the most unlikely of us, which is why Abraham Lincoln remains the supreme example of great leadership. A great leader, said Emerson, exhibits new possibilities to all humanity. "We feed on genius. . . . Great men exist that there may be greater men."

Great leaders, in short, justify themselves by emancipating and empowering their followers. So humanity struggles to master its destiny, remembering with Alexis de Tocqueville: "It is true that around every man a fatal circle is traced beyond which he cannot pass; but within the wide verge of that circle he is powerful and free; as it is with man, so with communities." ●

# 1

# Hugo Chávez in the News

SINCE HIS ELECTION TO VENEZUELA'S PRESIDENCY IN 1998, HUGO CHÁVEZ has claimed that the United States plans to assassinate him or to invade Venezuela or both. In August of 2005, Christian broadcaster Pat Robertson indeed called for President Chávez's assassination. Robertson said of Chávez:

"He has destroyed the Venezuelan economy, and he's going to make that a launching pad for communist infiltration and Muslim extremism all over the continent [of South America] .... [I]f he thinks we're going to assassinate him, I think we really ought to go ahead and do it. It's a whole lot cheaper than starting a war, and I don't think any oil shipments will stop."

The U.S. response to this was mixed. In an editorial cartoon, Ed Stein depicted two Muslim men witnessing Pat Robertson's televised call for Chávez's death. One of them says to the other, "Christianity is a religion of peace—But it gets perverted by fundamentalist religious extremists!" The *Chicago*

Polarizing television evangelist Pat Robertson called for the assassination of Venezuelan president Hugo Chávez during the August 22, 2005, broadcast of his show *The 700 Club*. Robertson asserted that it is the duty of the United States to stop Chávez from making Venezuela a "launching pad for communist infiltration and Muslim extremism."

*Tribune* commented that Robertson was being "wacky." U.S. State Department spokesperson Sean McCormick said Robertson's remark had been "inappropriate." In a New York *Daily News* editorial headed "Rev's call to kill shames us all," Errol Louis said, rather more forcefully, that "wacky" and "inappropriate" are words to use when your uncle says silly things at the dinner table, *not* when the man who founded Christian broadcasting in the United States and who has ties to the White House calls for the assassination of the democratically elected leader of another country. When a Muslim leader calls for President Bush's death, Louis pointed out, we call that "terrorism," not "wacky."

But officials from the administration of President George W. Bush said only that assassination is not part of United States government policy. Criticized by numerous U.S. religious leaders, Robertson apologized: It is not right, he agreed, to call for an assassination. But was he sorry? He didn't seem to be, actually. In his apology he cited Protestant theologian Dietrich Bonhoeffer, who supported efforts in Nazi Germany to assassinate Adolf Hitler and was put to death for his involvement in that assassination attempt. Robertson and many others indeed see Chávez as a serious threat to the United States, calling him a dictator who "intends to fund the violent overthrow of democratically elected governments throughout South America."

President Chávez's own response to Robertson was only in part predictable. Chávez was, with some justice, able to say, I *told* you they want to assassinate me. He noted that the official response to Robertson's "terrorist remarks" was tepid. A few weeks later he said this with considerable force, when he told an American interviewer, "If the imperialist government of the White House dares to invade Venezuela, the war of 100 years will be unleashed in South America."

But just days after Robertson's remarks, Chávez offered to sell low-cost gasoline and heating oil to poor communities in the United States, including to Native American tribal communities. Robert Free Galvan, who spoke to Indian tribes concerning Chávez's offer, says that Chávez and others in Latin America seek "an alternative to the World Trade Organization [WTO], North American Free Trade Agreement [NAFTA]" and other economic organizations that "seem to favor the rich and powerful corporations. Chávez has spent billions of oil dollars on education, feeding and housing the people of his country." Previous governments, Galvan continued, "had channeled much of the country's resources into a few hands." Chávez, himself part indigenous and part black, born into a poor rural family that had not benefited from Venezuela's years of prosperity, wanted that to change.

A few weeks later, after Hurricane Katrina caused billions of dollars of damage to the coasts of Louisiana and Mississippi, Chávez became the first foreign leader to offer a massive aid package to the United States' Gulf Coast. President Chávez said

Venezuela would immediately send food, water, and a million extra barrels of petroleum (66,000 at reduced rates for poor communities affected by the storm) to its "North American brothers." Additionally, he offered mobile hospital units, medical personnel, and power generators, all of them badly needed by the people of that region. The Bush administration said no. The aid was in fact provided anyway, through the oil company CITGO, which is owned by Venezuela.

One key word that comes up repeatedly in discussions of President Chávez and his policies—and in the U.S. response to Chávez—is "oil." Venezuela's identity as the world's fifth largest producer of oil is critical to our understanding of the role of the country—and its leader—in modern politics.

After Chávez took office, he traveled around the world to meet with the other members of OPEC (the Organization of Petroleum Exporting Countries). He became the first world leader to visit Saddam Hussein since the 1991 Gulf War. It was one of many visits made in order to reconstitute OPEC and curtail the production of oil, raising the price of oil per barrel. Oil prices had, in the 1980s, been driven down when OPEC's control over production had faltered and the oil market was glutted. With the world supply of oil way up, its price dropped. This drop in price had been disastrous for Venezuela. Ninety percent of foreign exports and 75 percent of the government's income are based on oil money, and when the price of oil fell, Venezuela found itself unable to pay off its foreign debt. Its unit of currency, the bolivar, fell in value against foreign currencies by almost 90 percent between 1983 and 1988. In Venezuela, prices went up, unemployment rose, and such staples as salt, rice, and sugar were in short supply. Eventually, the banks failed. Chávez's success in urging OPEC to regulate oil production has increased the country's income to the point that it can fund his numerous programs, called "missions," for the poor, providing schools, medical care, and other essentials.

But the government of the United States (among others) doesn't like Chávez's friends. Not only did Chávez visit Iran and Iraq, he has also allied himself with Cuba's Fidel Castro and angered U.S. leaders by undermining the U.S. embargo on Cuban products. He is accused of harboring guerilla fighters from neighboring Colombia and refuses the United States' request to use Venezuela's air space in its war against drugs in Colombia. Some American critics go further, accusing Chávez of funding or even training Middle East terrorists.

All in all, relations between the United States and the current government of Venezuela could scarcely be worse. The United States has labeled Chávez a "negative force" in the region and fears his efforts to unite Latin American countries, a charge that has never been proved. When the shortest coup d'etat (forceful takeover of a government) in history removed Chávez from office for two days in 2002, the United States was quick to recognize the government that replaced him and has been accused, by Chávez, of aiding and abetting that coup. Nearly every other government in the Western Hemisphere condemned the coup. If the U.S. government has not attempted to assassinate him, as Chávez claims, then it has, at the least, contributed $5 million to his opponents (through National Endowment for Democracy, an organization funded through the U.S. Congress) in an effort to bring down his government. Yet Mr. Chávez was elected by a majority of 56.2 percent—the largest margin in Venezuela's history—in a democratic vote that was verified as accurate and honest by the Carter Center, managed (at that time) by former president Jimmy Carter.

Chávez, for his part, calls President Bush "Mr. Danger." Venezuelan television has broadcast recordings of U.S. criticisms of Chávez accompanied by the "evil empire" music from *Star Wars*. Chávez has likened capitalism to Frankenstein's monster, Count Dracula, Jack the Ripper, and the Boston Strangler. He adds that capitalists are worse. And in 2004, Chávez warned Washington that if the United States attempted

Hugo Chávez talks with Iraqi president Saddam Hussein in Baghdad, Iraq, on August 10, 2000. The Venezuelan president has been sympathetic to Iraq and its former leader, to the chagrin of the United States and its allies.

to kill him or to invade, he would indeed cut off oil shipments. In 2006, he again threatened to cease selling oil to the United States. It may be one of the times when a nation can in fact be said to have another "over a barrel"—in this case, many millions of barrels, all of them filled with oil.

So, who is this man who provokes assassination requests from a right-wing Christian leader and who seems to respond with the Christian virtue of "turning the other cheek," offering aid to the poor or hurricane-struck of the United States and calling them "brothers"? He is, for one thing, a man about whom it seems impossible to be neutral. Some people see him as an idealist, a socialist leader who will at long last free Venezuela's poor from a history of abuse and disempowerment that is as old as Spain's conquest of the land in the fifteenth century. His supporters point to his democratic election and his many social programs for the poor. They believe his personal history as the child of a poor rural family makes him able to genuinely represent his people. Others see him as a man who is on his way to becoming the latest in a long history of Venezuelan military dictators, citing human-rights violations, changes in the constitution that increase his power, and his laws that make it illegal to criticize him or his policies. Some people claim that he is actually insane.

In Venezuela, of course, the debates over Chávez's true identity—"Hugo the Messiah" or "Hurricane Hugo"—and his intentions are hotter than those in the United States. Before being elected in 1998, Chávez, a member of the Venezuelan military, had been jailed for leading a failed 1992 coup against then-president Carlos Andres Perez. He himself was the subject of that very short coup in 2002, as well as strikes and work stoppages. He is, the *New York Times* pointed out in 2002, a leader so controversial that construction workers and upper-class housewives in designer dresses have at times united against him. But it is the poor who elected Chávez and the poor who keep him in office, who supported his constitutional changes and voted "no" in the 2004 recall referendum that would have peacefully removed him from office. Venezuela is a country with an underclass so vast—about 80 percent of the country's 25 million people—that they can outvote the unions and the upper class. In Chávez they see the hope for a kind of social change—Chávez himself would say a revolution—that has never happened in Venezuela. He is not only from a poor background, he is *mestizo*—mixed race—like most of Venezuela's citizens. "Now poor Venezuelans look in the mirror and see a future president. That is what makes the elite feel threatened," a hardware-store clerk said to the *New York Times Magazine*.

That the debate is heated reflects the importance of what is at stake. Venezuela was a colony of Spain for 300 years and (most of the time) a military dictatorship after that. Democracy in Venezuela isn't very old, only about 40 years.

Chávez was democratically elected, but he has used the military to run many of his social programs and gives the military a role far larger than his predecessors. Venezuelans fear violence. The riots of 1989 (although they took place before Chávez's presidency), as well as the attempted coups and other violent protests, are reminders of how volatile their country can be. What's more, a military dictatorship would seem to many Venezuelans to be old fashioned: "Revolutions and coup d'etats are so yesterday," said a young dentist, who was educated in the United States, in a *New York Times Magazine* article. "It's really embarrassing for Venezuela."

Embarrassment aside, some Venezuelans fear Chávez's effect on the economy. Chávez has helped pass laws that allow the government to expropriate (take over) some of the land belonging to some of Venezuela's rich families and give it to the poor, arguing that it is wrong for the country to be importing more than 60 percent of its food while land lies fallow and farmers have no place to farm. He has taken over idle factories and turned them over to the workers to run. But such programs threaten the people who own and run big businesses in Venezuela and make them (as well as foreign investors) reluctant to invest their money there. Even before Chávez was elected, many of Venezuela's richer people took themselves and their money out of the country.

That the debate is heated reflects the importance of the issues, but that it is also colorful reflects the identity of the president himself, whose media presence is unsurpassed. Friends and foes agree that he is a natural showman. Having surrendered after leading the failed coup of 1992, Chávez was allowed 90 seconds on television in order to tell his coconspirators to lay down their weapons. It didn't take him the whole 90 seconds to capture the country's attention. In well under a minute, Chávez managed to rally support for his cause, saying that *por ahora* (for the moment) the coup had failed, thus suggesting that the next time it wouldn't. He became, with that

After attempting to overthrow Venezuela's government, Hugo Chávez (then a lieutenant colonel) was arrested and escorted by military intelligence officers on February 5, 1992.

one speech, a hero. Then, in 2002, appearing on television after the coup that failed to topple him, he told the cameras to back up so that viewers could see the portraits flanking him: Jesus on his right and, on his left, Simón Bolívar, his hero, the nineteenth-century liberator of several South American countries from Spain.

Since his election, Chávez has appeared on his own highly rated TV show, *Aló Presidente* (Hello President) on Sundays. He dresses casually, sometimes appearing in jeans and a bright red shirt. The show is unscripted. It starts at about 11:00 in the morning and ends whenever the president is done talking and taking calls, and, sometimes, playing video footage of himself traveling the country, visiting hospitals, schools, or ordinary people at work—at least once, that was eight hours later, long after his live audience, who are not permitted to leave, had given up hoping for a toilet break or a meal. On the show, the president talks about personal memories, sings or recites poetry, and discusses politics, Christianity, and (his first love) baseball. On one notable show, several of these subjects came together, as Chávez fired seven of the upper managers of the state-run oil company by hollering, "You're out!" and blowing an umpire's whistle.

He also keeps audiences informed about how his youngest daughter's pet turtle is doing.

*Aló Presidente* is watched intently by Chávez's followers, and also by his opponents, who seem to have a horrified fascination with it. He sings, he rambles, he speaks in sentence fragments, and—say those who disagree with him—the content of what he says seems to run out your ears or through your fingers, too liquid to argue with or even to identify. A competing show, *Aló, Ciudadanos!* (Hello, Citizens) does attempt to respond critically to Chávez's statements, but, says the station's owner, Alberto Revell, it is like keeping up with the Energizer Bunny.

It is not possible to know what the long-term outcome of Hugo Chávez's presidency will be, but it is possible to look at his history and the history of his country and understand how Venezuela produced a leader like Chávez.

# 2

# Hugo Chávez and Venezuelan History

**HUGO CHÁVEZ'S ELECTION AND HIS ROLE IN MODERN VENEZUELA CANNOT** be understood without knowing a little of Venezuela's history. President Chávez often refers to his country's history, such as when the new constitution he helped pass renamed the country "the Bolivarian Republic of Venezuela" and when he says his policies are part of a "Bolivarian revolution." "Bolivarian" is a reference to Simón Bolívar, an important leader of the nineteenth-century fight to free Venezuela (and many other Latin American countries) from Spanish rule.

The roots of modern Venezuelan politics go back as far as Spain's conquest of what is now Venezuela, in the 1400s, when, on August 8, 1498, four men from a tribe called the Caribs discovered Christopher Columbus, then on his third voyage to what Europeans would call the New World. Columbus called it *Tierra de Gracia*, "Land of Graces," because it was so beautiful. The Carib men no doubt had some of the same response to Europeans as many native peoples: they found the Europeans pale and hairy, and possessed of such oddities as pants, guns, and horses. Chávez once joked with a female interviewer who asked him about his hairless legs; he said they are hairless because of the Indians in his mixed racial heritage.

The initial Spanish conquest of Central and South America was made in search of riches. Even after explorers realized that they had failed to find a western route to the spices of India and the wealth that would have brought, they were looking for wealth rather than for a place to settle. The conquistadors—conquerors—wanted money and believed they would find gold in the New World. They found some, and gold is still one of Venezuela's exports, but they never found the great wealth they sought. They could not find it, because what they were looking for didn't exist. They sought a legend: "El Dorado," a kingdom where gold was so plentiful that the king wore gold dust rubbed into his body.

The Spanish conquest was a disaster for the many native peoples. The Spanish took what gold they could find, sometimes by violence, and forced the natives to dive for pearls off the island of Cubagua until the pearls ran out, carried some natives away, and shipped others off as slaves. Native people died in wars, of overwork, or of European diseases, especially smallpox, for which they had no inherited immunity. (Small pox killed many people of European extraction as well, but it was nearly always fatal to native tribal peoples.) One estimate is that the native population of South America was reduced by about 90 percent by the end of the conquest.

Yet, Spanish colonization differed from English colonization in one way that is crucial. Whereas the English seemed to have seen native peoples largely as an impediment to colonization and wished to remove them, the Spanish viewed them as a kind of "natural resource" and wished to keep them around and put them to work. It was partly a matter of attitudes towards

physical work: many people who write about the Spanish conquest note that the Spaniards who settled the (South) American
colonies believed that labor was menial and degrading and, to
this day, a middle-class Venezuelan man prefers not to have to
shine his own shoes.

By the middle of the 1500s, the Spanish had decided that
the real riches of the New World lay in its fertile lands. They
established haciendas, or plantations, for the exotic and valuable products they learned about from the New World's native
inhabitants. Many of the products we take for granted come,
of course, from the Americas, including chocolate, potatoes,
tomatoes, and corn. Tobacco, coffee, and sugar cane, from Asia,
also would be grown in huge amounts in the New World. In
the 1500s the most important of these would be something
Europeans had never seen before: cacao—chocolate—from
a tree they (very scientifically!) named in Latin, *Theobrama
cacao*, "food of the gods." Chocolate, in the form of hot chocolate, became, like coffee and tea, one of the high-class luxury
foods of Europeans.

The *encomienda* system that bound the natives to Spanish
settlers as laborers on plantations said that the natives had to
work as slaves for the Spanish but that the haciendas' owners
had to take care of them. In practice, this meant that the owners forced Christianity on native people, but did not take care
of them. Many died, though some escaped and ran away to the
llanos, the vast plains of central Venezuela. Beginning in the early
1500s, enslaved blacks from Africa were brought over both for the
mining of gold and copper and to work on cacao plantations.

By the mid-1600s, the most valuable Spanish exports were
cacao, tobacco, wheat, and animal hides from the herds of
cattle on the llanos. The cattle had been a European import: at
the time of the conquest, there were no horses or cattle native
to the Americas. (The Spanish also exported native people to
the island of Hispaniola—now the Dominican Republic and
Haiti—to work as slaves on the sugar plantations there.)

The most profitable export remained cacao, and the wealthiest people in Venezuela were the plantation owners in the fertile region that the Spanish called Caracas, now the country's capital and biggest city. They farmed mostly the one crop, and it was better than gold. Chocolate prices boomed. The rich plantation owners were variously called *mantuanos*, for the expensive clothes from Mantua, Spain, that the women wore, or, as a class, *Gran cacao*, for the source of their wealth. Racially, they were called *blancos*, or whites. The German Alexander von Humboldt said of them, "in no other part of Spanish America has civilization assumed a more European character." They seemed, he said, more European than Europeans.

Many people were *Criollas*, or Creoles, people of Spanish heritage born in the New World. Although many Criollas were wealthy, they were always likely to find themselves passed over for political appointments from Spain; these went to *peninsulars*, Spaniards born in Spain.

Lower in the social and financial hierarchy were the enslaved blacks. There were also a number of runaway blacks and Indians. Some of them went to the llanos region and became cowboys, herding cattle. It was a recognizable cowboy culture, with the hard work of herding cattle and the toughness and independence that goes along with that way of life. (Except when it was rainy season and they had to herd cattle from canoes, which is not what North Americans expect of cowboys!)

The majority of the population was mixed race, in part because few Spanish women settled in the New World. The offspring of Spaniards and natives were called mestizos; there were also zambos, of Indian and black parentage, and mulattoes, of black and white parentage—all of whom are sometimes called *pardos*—or "browns." Some estimates say that the population of Venezuela in 1700 was 45 percent pardo, 25 percent white, 15 percent Indian, and 15 percent black. In practice, it was probably even more mixed than that, since it is often impossible to know people's racial background by looking at them. This fact troubled the upper-class whites, who made laws that pardos had to wear different clothes than whites and couldn't study at the university. A popular motto said "Todo blanco es caballero" (Every white man is a gentleman). Pardos worked in trades, as laborers, or on cattle ranches. There was thus an established, legalized separation of people that largely corresponded with both race and class. All this would be important when it came to Venezuela's wars of independence from Spain.

In 1728, the Bourbon family of Spain, then in power, reorganized the colonial governmental and economic structure to make it more efficient and more profitable. Plantation owners had been defying Spain and trading with smugglers to avoid Spanish taxes. The Bourbons gave the Compañia Guipuzcoana (also known as the Caracas Company) a monopoly on cacao, which then gave them the power to set the price that would be paid to farmers for cacao, since there was no one else the farmers could sell it to.

Venezuela came to its revolution in a time of revolutions—those of the thirteen colonies (that would become the United States), of France, and of Haiti. And Venezuela revolted for reasons related to all of these. Its revolution was, in some ways, like that of the thirteen colonies, who wanted free trade and were impatient with overseas rulers that saw them as a cash cow. The French Revolution had less to do with trade and was more an uprising against an aristocracy. Haiti's revolution was a rebellion against slavery. Venezuela's revolutionaries were influenced by all of these. The different populations and the different agendas would make for a messy revolution and, ultimately, a messy postrevolutionary period. The black and brown majority, for instance, had no reason to believe they would be better off under local rule than under overseas rule by Spain.

Although there had been revolts against slave holders, the first protest by whites against Spain was in 1749, by a Creole

Philip V of Spain was the first Bourbon ruler of that country. The House of Bourbon ruled France, Spain, and Italy from as far back as the sixteenth century.

who lost his job to a peninsular. He was sent to prison. Black rebels of the same period were put to death.

A number of early uprisings and independence movements were put down easily. Venezuelan-born Francisco Miranda, for example, was inspired by the revolutionary spirit he had seen while living in France and America. He brought a force of Americans, English, French, and Irish volunteers to free his native country, then was startled to discover that the Venezuelan response was not to join the revolution but to call for Spanish soldiers to get rid of them.

What set off the Venezuelan independence movement with some seriousness was a change in administration in Spain: Venezuelans woke up one morning in 1810 to discover that they were a French colony instead of a Spanish one. Napoléon Bonaparte had defeated and imprisoned King Fernando VII of Spain, and Napoléon's brother Joseph was now their king. King Joseph sent replacement governments to all the Spanish colonies of the New World. None of the Spanish colonies were happy about this, but Venezuela's economic dependence on a single crop made it particularly vulnerable to the change in regime. If Venezuela became a French colony, then it would be, like France, at war with England. This was a problem because the English were Venezuela's best customers.

So, although there had been small rebellions, it can be said that the real independence movement began in Caracas with a group of angry plantation owners who did not want their trade with England disrupted. They were a small percentage of the population, so, almost from the beginning they had to consider what they would need to do to gain the support of the rest of the country. Very early in the movement, for instance, they called for an end to the slave trade—though not the freeing of the slaves—in an effort simultaneously to appease the pardos but not lose their workers.

The 1811 independence movement created a very short-lived "First Republic" of Venezuela. It also produced a civil war

King Joseph Bonaparte (1768-1844) ruled as the King of Naples from 1806 to 1808 and the King of Spain from 1808 to 1813. He was appointed by his brother, French emperor, Napoléon I.

with those people who were loyal to Spain. The loyalists said that the March 12, 1812, earthquake in Caracas was proof that God was angry at the rebels. The loyalists and a Spanish army of 230 men defeated Francisco Miranda (who had tried for independence in 1806) and a 28-year-old named Simón Bolívar. Miranda would die in a Spanish prison; Bolívar was allowed to go into exile.

The Venezuelan independence movement was the first in Latin America, but not by long. In New Granada (now Colombia), Bolívar was able to raise an army of 70 men. Collecting troops as they traveled, the army retook Caracas. It was during this 1813 campaign that Bolívar was given the title "Liberator," by which he is still known in many countries of Latin America he helped to free. Bolívar created and commanded Venezuela's "Second Republic," its second government. This one wouldn't last long either.

In 1814, llaneros troops—Indians, pardos, and slaves—led by José Tomás Boves fought against Bolívar and his troops. Boves had been turned down for a "command post" by the revolutionaries, possibly because he was perceived as too rough and low class for them. He was white but not a gentleman. Promising freedom to the slaves, he gathered a mixed-race force. Although there were blacks, whites, Indians, and mixed-race people on both sides of the war, Boves addressed but also exploited the racial tensions of the country. He brought a different kind of anger to the war, encouraging his troops to do as the Spanish general Monteverde had the year before: destroy farms and houses, loot, rape, and pillage.

In Spain, the Royalists had finally expelled Napoléon's army, and Fernando VII was back in power. In 1815, he sent 10,000 troops under the command of General Pablo Morillo to Venezuela. This should have been a crushing force, except that he found himself fighting Boves's llaneros forces. Boves himself had died in battle, but when his troops tried to join up with Morillo, he told them he had no use for them, thus repeating the error that the revolutionaries had made with Boves himself. As a result, they fought against him instead of with him, using tactics that Morillo knew from the Spanish resistance to Napoléon. The llaneros troops did not march in formation but rather fought with guerilla (literally "small war") methods, setting ambushes and fighting in small groups with whatever weapons they could get.

One new leader of the llaneros was named Manuel Piar, a mulatto man. As historian Geoffrey Fox has said, "The black, mulatto, and Indian soldiers in the liberation armies had a different stake in the war than the whites. For them it was not enough to replace Spanish rulers with *mantuanos*. They demanded a more open society, and symbolic of that openness would be the abolition of slavery." We might argue that the demand for the abolition of slavery was more than a symbol.

Bolívar, while denying that racial differences had caused the domestic strife in America (meaning his America), visited Haiti, where enslaved blacks had risen up and defeated Napoléon's armies. Haiti's president, Alexandre Péhon, gave Bolívar weapons and ships, with Bolívar agreeing that he would free Venezuela's slaves.

In 1819, Bolívar established Venezuela's Third Republic, although the fighting would continue. The final battle was the defeat of the Spanish by Bolívar, Santiago Marino, and José Antonio Páez at Carabobo, near Valencia. Venezuela's independence had been accomplished by people of different races and countries fighting for different reasons. The last Royalist troops would not be expelled until 1823, by Páez.

Bolívar would go on to fight for the freedom of other South American countries and unite them very briefly into *Gran Colombia* (Greater Colombia), which included Venezuela, New Granada (Colombia), Panama (then a part of New Granada), Ecuador, Peru, Bolivia, and part of Chile. He was, also briefly, the president of Gran Colombia and the dictator of Peru. Bolívar hoped to unite countries from Mexico to Argentina, but his

South American revolutionary leader Simón Bolívar (1783–1830) is the subject of this nineteenth century painting. Bolívar led the fight for independence in Venezuela and is celebrated as a hero there.

vision of a united South America failed. Bolívar traveled great distances trying to preserve the unity of Gran Colombia, but Venezuela was the first country to secede from Gran Colombia, under the leadership of José Antonio Peréz. Bolívar, who would eventually be again called Liberator, whose statue would be erected in town squares and his picture put on people's walls like that of a saint,  found himself demonized and the target of assassination attempts by ex-allies. In 1830, he resigned as president of Gran Colombia and dictator of Peru and went into exile. He died later that year having declared, "[South] America is ungovernable. Those in service of the revolution have plowed the seas." Venezuelan crowds proclaimed, "The tyrant is dead." Geoffrey Fox says, poignantly, "He had destroyed the world he knew. . . by destroying the colonial system and he could not understand or accept the new world he had helped create."

# 3

# After the Revolution

**THE REVOLUTION HAD GONE ON FOR 20 YEARS AND HAD LEFT VENEZUELA** in chaos. There had been little schooling. Crops and industries had been destroyed. For a generation, there had been only war. There had been no stable government.

General José Antonio Páez formed a government, Venezuela's Fourth Republic, in 1830. It went against everything that Bolívar had fought for and believed in, and against everything the mestizos and pardos had fought for.

Páez ruled as the first of Venezuela's *caudillo* dictators. The term is often translated as "strong man," but it also means something like "war chief." By the end of the war, in the absence of a central government, Venezuela was ruled by local caudillos, and there was no legal mechanism to create the sort of government that Bolívar and others had fought for. The people of Venezuela had no experience with a government of their own or a government they could trust. Páez had been a caudillo before he

## IT IS THE TRADITION OF CAUDILLO RULERS THAT FUELS THE FEARS OF HUGO CHÁVEZ'S OPPONENTS, WHO SEE IN HIM A HARKENING BACK TO THAT MODE OF RULE.

was a general; he would now be the country's caudillo, strong enough—he had been called the Tiger of the Llanos during the war—and, as ruler, rich enough to keep the lesser caudillos at least somewhat in line. The tradition of caudillo rulers is one that would flourish over the next century and a half, and it is the tradition that fuels the fears of Chávez's opponents, who see in him a harkening back to that mode of rule.

So a war that had been fought, at least by some, in the hopes of changing the social order resulted in the 17-year rule (1830–1847) of a military dictator and the reestablishment of a rich, white, increasingly urban elite in the Caracas region. It seemed all that had changed was that their wealth now came from coffee instead of cacao. The cacao plantations had been destroyed in the fighting, and coffee would be a more immediately profitable crop, requiring only about five years, instead cacao's eight or ten, to be fruitful. Also coffee had become more profitable than cacao. So, the dependence on one crop would be replaced by the dependence on another. And, again, it would be more profitable for most people to work on coffee plantations than to work their own small farms, so it was a system that somewhat discouraged people from owning and maintaining small independent farms.

Páez, or people virtually appointed by Páez, would rule until 1847. They were, as a group, called the Conservative Oligarchy. They stood for a strong central government and supported the old privileges of the church and of the upper class.

Then, in the 1840s, coffee prices fell worldwide. Many wealthy planters found themselves with debts they couldn't

General Jose A. Páez (1790–1873) was General in Chief during the Venezuelan War of Independence from 1811 to 1812. Regarded as a hero for his part in liberating Venezuela, Páez went on to lead the country as president.

pay. An opposition to Páez formed that, in part, consisted of planters who wanted him to create policies that would help them not lose everything. The liberal opposition believed in voting rights for all men, the separation of church and state, and a somewhat decentralized government, with states and provinces having more power than the conservatives allowed them.

But opposition leader Antonio Leocadio Guzmán also appealed to some of the llaneros, including the man who would be (along with Bolívar and Bolívar's teacher, Simón Rodriguez) one of Hugo Chávez's heroes: Ezequiel Zamora. He called himself the General of the Sovereign People. His slogans were "Land and free men," "general elections," and "Hatred toward the oligarchy." He sometimes used the cry of the French revolutionaries, "liberty, equality, and fraternity." One of his actions was to order the burning of the building in Barinas in which land titles were stored, so that when the poor seized land, as he wanted them to, there would be no records to help the land owners get it back. That was Zamora at his most extreme. But additionally, he believed in policies that would have dramatically—but less drastically—helped the very poor people of the Venezuelan countryside. He wanted a certain amount of land around each town to be available for common use, like the "commons" of old English or American towns, where everyone could allow their animals to graze, and like the land allotted for many years to English peasants, on which they could raise the food they needed to survive. And he wanted large landowners to provide ten milking cows to be grazed on common land to provide milk for the poor, many of whom couldn't have afforded cows even with free grazing. Exiled after a number of military defeats, Zamora returned to Venezuela in February of 1859 and fought until he was assassinated ten months later.

Hugo Chávez admires Zamora's goals, seeing him as someone who continued the fight for Bolívar's goals, including an end to slavery (which was ended in 1854, largely out of fear of slave uprisings) and Latin American unity.

Páez's dictatorship had been harsh, yet it had also been stable. What followed was not stable at all. Zamora's rebellions were just some of the wars and rebellions that tore Venezuela apart for the rest of the nineteenth and the beginning of the twentieth centuries. Although the failure of some plantations moved money into the hands of bankers and merchants, power remained in the hands of a relatively small percentage of the population, and there was never a break for long in the line of military dictators.

The governments changed often, but one that lasted was that of Guzmán Blanco (1870–1888). He was accepted as a genuine aristocrat on the grounds that his feet were so small that he could wear his wife's slippers. (Bolívar, too, had been admired for his tiny feet.) The relative stability of his regime was based largely on the era: the world market was strong, so coffee, cattle, and cacao prices were high, and foreign investors had money to invest in such things as Venezuelan railroads. He built boulevards in Caracas like those he admired in Paris, where he spent a great deal of time and a great deal of money, most of it stolen from the Venezuelan people. He had sewers and electricity installed in Caracas, a water supply piped in, and a public transportation system created. Guzmán Blanco became a rich, rich man, yet because times were good economically, he was able to stay in power until 1888.

Later caudillos would have a harder time maintaining their power, mostly because coffee prices fell again. It was not until 1908 that Venezuela would again have a stable government, and that was under Juan Vincente Gómez, vice president to his predecessor, a barely literate dictator who took over the country in a military coup and ruled for 27 years, from 1908 to 1935. He is infamous in Venezuelan history for his corruption and greed, for seizing any land he wanted, and any women. (He never married but is believed to have fathered more than 100 children.) Some of the land seized may have been that of Hugo Chávez's great grandfather, Pedro Perez Delgado (nicknamed "Maisanta"), who led an uprising against Vincente Gómez that failed to unseat the dictator. As president, Chávez expropriated the land, an estate called La Marquesena in Barinas. It remains unclear if his ancestor owned it or worked on it. Since Chávez believes that workers should own the land they farm or the factories they work in, it may not be a distinction that is important to him.

Reading any historical discussion of Vincente Gómez's rule is a useful, confusing, revealing, and alarming exercise in understanding Venezuela's history. Gómez was, by any measure, a tyrant, a monster. People danced in the street when he died (peacefully, in his bed, at age 78). He stole, raped, and tortured Venezuela's citizens at will. Some of those tortured were 17- and 18-year-old students who, in 1928, began a strike against him that led to a failed military revolt against the government. (After his death, 14 tons of shackles used on prisoners were thrown into the sea). But, say historians, with wonder, he did at least manage to create and maintain a stable government. That continued to be regarded as something of a miracle.

Critically, for Venezuela's future, Gómez oversaw and encouraged the extraction and sale of petroleum, which was the real "gold" of Venezuela. Even more than cocoa or coffee had been, oil would become a single "crop" on which the economy would depend, bringing unimaginable wealth into the country, but bringing it only to some people and eliminating (as less profitable) other ways of making a living.

Venezuela had always known it had oil—at least it knew it had something that was black and sticky and useful for patching leaky roofs. But in the early 1900s, with the invention of the automobile (and airplane and other vehicles with combustion motors), gasoline was going to be in such heavy demand that crude oil was called "black gold."

At first, Venezuela, under Gómez's leadership, had foreign companies such as Royal Dutch Shell and Standard Oil of New Jersey (which would become Exxon) pay for the right to drill for oil and take it away, mostly from the shore of Lake Maracaibo. The Venezuelans didn't see any reason to process the oil in their own country. They didn't have refineries or people trained to run refineries. And they didn't, at that time, care what happened to the natural gas that is now a valuable byproduct of oil refining. The money they received was plenty, seemingly unlimited money for something they weren't using anyway. Venezuelans had their new single crop, and they didn't even have to grow this one. The government had money to pay for roads and the army and to line the dictator's pockets. In 1929, Venezuela was the largest exporter of oil in the world (and would be until 1970), and oil money would keep the country rich during the world depression of the 1930s.

Oil urbanized the country as small farmers and landless laborers began to work in the company towns that grew up around the oil. The rich grew very rich indeed, and there also came to be an urban middle class. This was new. But while the country became rich, most of its people remained very poor. With a growing middle class and the coming of unions for workers, there was more resistance to Gómez, but his access to oil money and the national army it paid for kept them in check.

By the time of Gómez's death in 1935, the country was, in some ways, modern. It had a centralized government with a strong army—strong enough that small caudillos and their followers could no longer threaten it. At Gómez's death, that army produced the new government by appointing as the country's leader General Eleazer López Contrerar, the man who had been Gómez's minister of war and the navy. During the next two regimes, Venezuela began to modernize politically and economically. It increased the amount of money the country collected from foreign oil companies to 30 percent and instituted an income tax and social security. It also passed an agrarian reform law designed to distribute government land to small farmers who had none. But it was still a government created and supported by the military, and of a population of 3.5 million, 90 percent were illiterate. Roads were dirt and there was no public health system.

When the opposition party, the Acción Democrática (Democratic Action) party, decided that it was time for a democratic government, they organized and carried out a coup d'etat. (This somewhat dubious approach to establishing a democracy is something that Chávez supporters point to when his opponents claim that Chávez's 1992 attempted coup proves that he doesn't believe in democracy.) Novelist Romulo Betancourt became president in October 1945 and tried to establish reforms. He wanted to give back land that Gómez had taken from people and to create small farms again. It was not until 1947 that a president was elected by the people of Venezuela and that president, the novelist Rómulo Gellegos, remained in power for less than a year before, in November 1948, the military took over the government again.

Between 1948 and 1958, Venezuela was ruled by General Marcos Pérez Jiménez. When Pérez Jiménez attempted to get himself elected democratically in 1952, he ran into some problems. He wanted there to be a vote for a general assembly that would then choose a president: him. But people didn't want to vote because they had no reason to trust the democratic process, so he made it mandatory to register and to vote. Then, when the elected assembly did vote for a candidate and—as the votes were being counted—someone else seemed to be winning, he simply declared himself the winner and told people to stop counting the ballots. They stopped.

Pérez Jiménez's rule has been described as one of "massive public works and heavy repression." There remained limitless oil money with which to build highways and public

Dictator Marcos Pérez Jiménez was president of Venezuela from 1952 to 1958. Venezuela's economy developed rapidly during his term, but he was forced from office and lived in exile in the United States until he was extradited to Venezuela on embezzlement charges.

buildings, many of them too badly planned to be of use. Shopping centers and office buildings remained empty; a "cloverleaf" entrance to the highway was so complicated that it acquired a nickname: the octopus. He did not provide money for better public education or public health.

Pérez Jiménez was deposed on January 23, 1958, by a combination of a general strike in Caracas and a rebellion led by the air force. He flew to Miami, Florida. Hugo Chávez was four years old.

In November of 1958, Romulo Betancourt of Acción Democrática was elected president by a popular vote, but people on all sides wished to force him from office. Pérez Jiménez's supporters got funding from the dictator of the Dominican Republic. Opponents on the left fought a continuous guerilla war. One of them, Douglas Bravo, would later become a friend of Chávez's brother Adan, though ultimately an opponent of Hugo Chávez. Fuernas Armadas de Liberacíon Nacional (Armed Forces of the National Liberation), encouraged by the Cuban revolution of 1959, hoped for a more left-wing government. Additionally, in 1962, leftwing parts of Venezuela's national guard and the marine corps revolted, wanting Betancourt to nationalize the oil industry. Betancourt believed he could work with the United States, which was Venezuela's biggest customer and which also owned most of the oil companies doing business in the country at the time. In 1954, the CIA had overthrown a leftist government in Guatemala, so Betancourt had reason to believe he was better off working with the United States and its interests than against it. Indeed, U.S. president John Kennedy would supply Betancourt with the missiles he used to defend himself during the marine corps mutiny in Puerto Cabrella.

Chávez, born in 1954, was thus born into a world in which democracy had made few inroads, and into a part of the country and a class that had not benefited from Venezuela's great wealth. The democracy that did develop would succeed by

Venezuelan president Romulo Betancourt, who served from 1945 to 1948 and again from 1959 to 1964, is shown at the United Nations General Assembly in 1963.

some measures, and fail by others, which is what he came to address as he grew up and examined the political process and the economics of his country.

The history of Venezuela's independence and of its dictators—and of the role of the military in the government—gives us a sense of the country's governments and their relation to the people. Other Latin American countries have similar histories, although Venezuela's oil has always set it apart. American or English critics of Chávez's democracy make a mistake when they compare what is happening there now only with some idealized form of the democracy in the United States. (After all, in 2000, the United States elected a president who received fewer popular votes than the loser.) We can also see why Venezuela might have mixed feelings about the United States. During its days as a colony, Venezuela had been a source of income for Spain. What people living there wanted for themselves was—by the laws of Spain—less important than what Spain needed from them. It is easy for them to resent being seen only as a source of oil for other parts of the world.

And it was always a country deeply divided by race and class.

# 4

# Enter Hugo Chávez

**HUGO CHÁVEZ WAS BORN ON JULY 28, 1954, IN THE LLANOS REGION OF** Venezuela, that low, flat region that historically has been the land of cattle, cowboys, and rebels. But his parents weren't ranchers or cowboys—they were elementary school teachers living outside the small town of Sabareta in the state of Barinas. His father dropped out of school after sixth grade, which was not unusual for a child of poor parents in rural Venezuela. What is less usual is that he later was able to go back to school and get the credentials he needed to teach.

Hugo Rafael Chávez Frías (to call him by his whole name) was the second child born to Hugo de los Reynes Chávez and Elena Frías de Chávez. His older brother is named Adan (Adam), and Chávez says that if he himself had been a girl, his mother planned to name him Eva, so that they would be Adam and Eve. As it turned out, he was named for his father and his mother's grandfather. He also bears his mother's

Hugo Chávez was born in the state of Barinas, shown above, into a poor family that stressed the importance of education to succeed in life.

maiden name, Frías, as the last part of his own, as is common in Latin America.

Both parents encouraged the children—Adan, Hugo, and four younger ones—to study hard, become educated, and then use that education as a means of getting out of Sabareta and out of poverty. It was an ambitious goal for them to have, since even on the salaries of two teachers, the family was poor.

It would be, however, a goal they were able to achieve: Adan became a university professor before his younger brother became involved in politics, and Hugo's other siblings became an electrical engineer, a banker, an English teacher, and a businessman. Hugo Chávez's father, Hugo Senior, became governor of the state of Barinas in 1998. The intelligence and energy that enabled his father to go back to school and become a teacher clearly was passed along—genetically and by example—to the children.

The family's house was, Chávez once said, "made of palm leaves." At other times, he elaborates and says it was a house of wattle and daub walls (mud mixed with straw, called *bahareque*), a dirt floor, with a roof of palm leaves, like thatching. It was the most common kind of house in Venezuela, in a style hundreds or perhaps thousands of years old, and had no electricity or running water.

Hugo, like his older brother, was born in the house of his father's mother, Rosa Inés, in the town of Sabareta proper. Her house was no better equipped than the parents' house, but at least in town there was a midwife to help at the birth. His mother's mother, Martha, lived in the town of Los Rastojos, which seemed a city to him simply because its little power plant could generate the electricity for two hours of light in the evening.

Both Adan and Hugo were raised by grandmother Rosa Inez, whom Hugo called Mama Rosa. The house was in town, yet cattle grazed nearby, and mangos, palms, avocados, papayas, and other trees grew all around. After the Chávezs' third son, Narcisco, was born, the family moved into Sabareta, not 150 feet from Mama Rosa's house. There the boy's father and mother built a small house of cement blocks with an asbestos roof and a cement floor. Hugo and Adan continued to live with their grandmother. If Chávez minded this or felt rejected by his parents he does not say so. He speaks fondly of fishing with his father early in the morning at the nearest river. But he credits his grandmother with raising him, with teaching him "to read, to work, to be honorable."

He says he liked to work hard, although Adan (the one who grew up to be a college professor) preferred to read. By the age of eight, Hugo helped to sow and harvest the corn, to clean the yard, and to help make and sell the coconut buns and papaya cakes his grandmother baked. Hugo gathered the green papaya, then they peeled, seeded, and chopped them up, and Mama Rosa cooked them in sugar to make a sweet snack called "spiders," which Hugo would sell at school. His grandmother would give him a small share of the money, which he kept in his plastic piggybank. He would also go where people were playing bolo (which is a kind of bowling), or to cock fights (where people bet on the outcome of fights between trained roosters, usually fitted with metal blades on their feet), or to festivals for the patron saint of the village. All of these are the common entertainments and festivals of Venezuela and the rest of Latin America. Hugo also picked and sold oranges to the local ice-cream maker, and Mama Rosa was generous about making sure the boys got lots of ice cream, which Hugo loved.

It was a childhood of hard work and little money, so that the boys went to school in ratty clothing and home-made sandals or, in high school, in old rubber boots. But Chávez doesn't speak of having been unhappy. He seems to have been secure in his grandmother's love, happy to be with her while she watered (and talked to) her plants and he sang to them. He also liked Mexican movies and a popular kind of music from Mexico called *rancheros*, and *llaneros*, the folk music of the people of the plains.

With his mother, Hugo had a more difficult and rebellious relationship. Once, when she was going to hit him with a stick—he doesn't say for what or if this was a typical punishment of that time and place—he grabbed the stick away from her and then ran away to the mountains. He disagreed with his mother about other things than her hitting him, though.

She wanted him to be a priest, and he obediently served for one year as an altar boy, cleaning the church's statues of Jesus and the saints, helping at Mass, and ringing the church bells. He did this last task so enthusiastically that everyone could tell when it was the little Chávez boy ringing the bells. He was a child of great energy and enthusiasms and very strong likes and dislikes, and as much as he enjoyed bell ringing, he came to dislike other things about the church. He especially disliked the way his church depicted Jesus as a meek victim. He believed in another reading of the Bible, one that is shared by many other Christians, which emphasizes the Jesus who was a rebel, a "revolutionary," Chávez says. Jesus overturned the power structure of his people, criticized the leaders, condemned corruption, and spoke often and passionately about taking care of the poor. That distinction—believing in Christianity while often being angry at the clergy (whom he has been known to call "devils in vestments")—remains.

As a child, Hugo heard something that disturbed him a lot. His grandmother Martha, while scolding Hugo's mother, said she was willful: "Elena, you are like that because you are an offshoot of that murderer, your grandfather. Rafael's father, he was a murderer. He killed a man. . . . [H]e tied him to a tree and shot him, and he cut off another man's head right in front of his children." That would indeed be a disturbing (though perhaps also exciting) thing to hear as a child. But it wasn't something that anyone would talk to him about. It was only later, as a young man, that Hugo learned that his great-grandfather was Pedro Perez Delgado, who, from 1914 until his capture in 1922, fought against the dictatorship of General Juan Vicente Gómez. Chávez would come to see his great-grandfather as a hero guerilla fighter, rather than as a murderer, but that wasn't how he was brought up. His parents did not speak proudly of the guerilla fighter in their family. Coming to understand another way of interpreting his great grandfather's actions "contributed a lot to who I am today," Chávez has said. He was also interested in a less controversial rebel, Simón Bolívar, who is almost considered a saint by many Latin American people.

At age 12, Chávez was in many ways a typical boy of his time and place, although he was unusual in that he stayed in school even though it required him to move to the bigger town of Bolinas for high school. Like the majority of Venezuelans, he is of mixed racial origins, with a blond (although mixed race) mother and a father who is of both black and Indian descent. He was a thin boy, with feet so big that his classmates called him "Triblin," the Spanish name for the Disney character Goofy. He was, however, unusually creative and strong willed. Many children dislike it when the doctor gives them shots, but Chávez says it took his father and three men to hold him down for his vaccinations. "I was both a coward and a rebel," he has said. But does he say proudly or ruefully? It's hard to tell. He liked to paint and sculpt (and won prizes for his artwork and also for a play he wrote) and used to get jobs singing at children's birthday parties.

Like most Venezuelan boys, Hugo preferred baseball to all other sports, even though as a child he and his friends had to play with a rubber ball and use a wooden plank as a bat. Baseball, brought to Venezuela in the late 1890s by rich young men who were attending American boarding school, is Venezuela's national sport, as it is in Cuba, the Dominican Republic, Nicaragua, and Panama. In most Central and South American countries people are passionate about soccer. It is a little thing but it is important. The countries that love baseball are the countries that looked to the United States for their model during the late 1800s, rather than to Europe. It is one small part in the complex relationship that has existed between Venezuela and the United States historically.

Chávez was more than just a baseball fan. One of his greatest heroes was Nestor Isaís "Látigo" Chavez (no relation), a Venezuelan who pitched for the major league San Francisco Giants. Hugo Chávez was a good pitcher himself. One trait that

Caracas, the capital of Venezuela, was the city where Chávez attended military school. In 1958, an angry mob attempted to attack the Municipal Police Headquarters.

is consistent in his character is that he works hard and usually does well at everything he attempts, and he dreamed of one day being a major league pitcher in the United States like his hero. When Hugo was 14 years old, Látigo died in a plane crash, and Hugo was so upset that he missed two days of school. Five years later, Hugo was still writing about Látigo in his diary—a long time for a teenager to remain loyal to a hero.

Later, in 1974, as a young man in the military academy in Caracas, Chávez would note in his diary that Venezuela didn't have a strong enough sense of its own identity. Even his beloved baseball came from America, of whose policies he was already critical, yet that couldn't make him love baseball any less, then or now.

Chávez would later say that for boys like him to have to leave home for high school makes it too hard for young people to continue with their schooling. Some of his government policies are based on the desire to make small farming towns easier to live in, make a living in, be educated in, and get good medical care in. But he graduated from the Daniel Florencio O'Leary School with a degree in science. In Venezuela, as in many countries in Europe, students begin to specialize in a subject while still in high school, choosing to focus on science or classics or to begin work in some less academic field.

Politically, Chávez was influenced by two of his best friends. They were the sons of a man named Jose Ruiz, who had been jailed for being a communist by the military dictator Marcos Pérez Jiménez. The first books Chávez read on communism and socialism may have come from the household of the Ruiz family.

# 5

# Toward
# a Revolution

WHEN THE 17-YEAR-OLD HUGO DECIDED TO ATTEND THE VENEZUELAN
Academy of Military Sciences in Caracas, it was not because he
was interested in a career in the military. Rather, he had been
advised that the academy was his best path toward a career in
major league baseball. As it turned out, the military academy
suited him. A bit self conscious from having come from a tiny
rural town, he seemed "shy and well mannered" to his classmates, but also "likeable and articulate."

Chávez was still a skinny guy with big feet. People who knew
him then say he wasn't handsome and he had trouble getting
girlfriends. When one girl rebuffed him and hurt his feelings, he
took a rotting donkey's head that he had found by the side of the
road and deposited it on her doorstep. (It is the sort of story that
appeals to people who are interested in Hugo Chávez's character:
he seems, throughout his life, to be proud, impulsive, and—at
times—quick tempered.)

President Salvador Allende committed suicide before he could be captured in a coup led by General Augusto Pinochet on September 11, 1973. Above, soldiers and firefighters carry Allende's body out of his destroyed presidential palace.

He majored in army engineering, played baseball, and, for a time, had his own local radio station. He even emceed a beauty contest. His studies also included political science, history, and "Marxism-Leninism," and he pursued his boyhood interest in Simón Bolívar. He and his friends began to speak of "Bolivarianism" and to dream of a united Latin America. And it would be a Latin America that helped the poor. (Douglas Bravo, the guerilla fighter who was a friend of Hugo's brother Adan, had also spoken of Bolivarianism. It is not an idea that began only with Chávez.)

People speak of Chávez's political awakening, a time when political issues really came alive for him. The writer Gabriel García Márquez (who has written novels about Simón Bolívar and dictator Juan Vincente Gómez) says that Chávez's political awakening came with the assassination of Chile's president Salvador Allende in September of 1973. The overthrow of an

## BY THE TIME HUGO CHÁVEZ GRADUATED FROM THE MILITARY ACADEMY IN 1975, HE HAD BEGUN TO THINK ABOUT THE NEED FOR THE MILITARY TO HAVE A ROLE IN RUNNING THE COUNTRY.

elected president by military officers shocked him into thinking about the modern political situation.

At 19, Chávez says, he saw Carlos Andrés Pérez inaugurated as president, and he says he wrote in his diary, "Watching him pass, I imagined myself walking there with the weight of my country on my own shoulders." If that is true, it is the only evidence that Chávez was thinking so early about becoming involved in the political process.

Richard Gott, author of the first book about Chávez in English, said Chávez was first politicized by his 1974 visit to Peru to celebrate the 150th anniversary of Peruvian independence from Spain, which came about after an 1824 battle in which Bolívar fought. In 1968, Peru had been seized by a left-wing military regime that began to try to reshape the country in ways that would influence Chávez later on. Peruvian president Juan Velasco Alvarado (president from 1968 to 1975) gave each of the visiting cadets and young officers a booklet of his speeches, called *The Peruvian National Revolution*, which Chávez treasured. Chávez saw a "strong bond" between the Peruvian people and their military, and he admired it. By the time he graduated from the military academy in 1975 with a degree in military arts and sciences, he had begun to think about the need for the military to have a role in running the country.

And yet, with his father's interest in politics, his own boyhood enthusiasm for Bolívar, and his school friends with whom he read about communism, he must have thought about politics all along. It was inescapable. Still, as when he interpreted his great-grandfather Perez Delgado as a freedom fighter rather than as a murderer, he would come to disagree with his family about politics for a time. He wouldn't talk with his family about politics when he was a cadet. His father had become a member of COPEI, the more conservative of the two main political parties.

As a young man, Chávez began a book about his great-grandfather and started to travel from town to town looking for documents in libraries and archives and talking to people about the stories that were told about the guerilla fighters of that time. He told Gabriel García Márquez that it was while traveling to do this research that he inadvertently crossed Venezuela's border into neighboring Colombia, where he was promptly arrested as a spy. The camera, photographs of the area, maps, and tape recorder that he carried could easily have been the tools of a spy, and how could he prove otherwise? He was interrogated for hours and "nearly exhausted." Then, as he and his interrogator sat, deadlocked, under a portrait of Simón Bolívar, Chávez thought of what to say. "Look, my captain, the way life is: just a century ago we were a single army, and that fellow who is watching us from the painting was the commander of us both. How could I be a spy?" His interrogator began to speak of Bolívar's dream of a Gran Colombia, and the two men wound up drinking beer in a bar together. The next day, a hungover Chávez was sent home across the border with a big hug. It is a very Chávez story, his using Bolívar and his quick, convincing arguments to get out of trouble and make a pal of an enemy. (Critics of Chávez—or anyone interest in logic—might note that his argument was a lousy one: even though the two countries have a historical tie to Bolívar, Chávez could still have been a spy.)

In 1977, Hugo Chávez married Nancy Colmenares, a woman from his hometown of Sabareta. She continued to live there while Chávez served in the military. He told Herma Marksman, a friend and lover, that he could not marry her, that "his mother would not give him permission to divorce Nancy." Several people who know Chávez have suggested that his mother wielded a fair amount of power over him, especially since she did not raise him. During his marriage to Nancy, which lasted 18 years, the couple had three children: Rosa Virginia, Maria Gabriela, and Hugo Rafael. Chávez seems to have nothing to say about the marriage, except that he was away a lot, and that they parted amicably. Herma Marksman, who was his girlfriend for 9 or 10 years, later wrote a book called *Chávez Used Me*, in which she claimed that she helped him with his thesis (to graduate from the military academy) and ran errands and carried messages for him during the early days of his political conspiracies. He is, she says, a man without loyalty, who makes use of people and then drops them.

After his graduation, Chávez was assigned to a counterinsurgency battalion in Barinas, putting down the last of the guerilla uprisings. In 1976, he was sent to Cumaná to stop a rebellion. There, he found himself shocked and disgusted by the treatment of the guerilla fighters. Awakened by the yells of prisoners being beaten with baseball bats (wrapped in cloth so they wouldn't leave marks), Chávez said there would be no torture under his command. Although he was threatened with a court martial for arguing with a superior officer, it was never carried out.

Chávez began to wonder where his loyalties really lay. During the same mission, he says, he watched while soldiers wounded in the fighting lay dying, begging him not to let them die. He wondered, "What am I doing here? On one side peasants in military uniforms torture peasant guerillas, and on the other peasant guerillas kill peasants dressed in green." It all seemed senseless to him. The people killing one another had more in common than not: they were poor and they had no real power, although some carried guns.

It was an awakening to Chávez—one of those moments when something becomes clear for the first time, when things that one has believed suddenly look different. Twenty-three years old, he organized the Liberation Army of the Venezuelan People. It was a very small organization with—he jokes—fewer members than there were words in the organization's name. "We hadn't the least idea at that time what we were going to do," he admits, except "to prepare ourselves in case something happened." He met another officer, Jesús Urdaneta Hernández, who soon became a friend, and Chávez told him about the revolutionary group. They thought of it as an alternative to the guerilla movement, an organization within the army.

In 1980, Chávez went back to the military academy in Caracas as a sports instructor, once again able to pursue his love of baseball. He also became a teacher of military history and politics there. The man who would be Venezuela's defense minister during Chávez's attempted coup in 1998 taught with him at the academy during the early 1980s and remembers Chávez as a good speaker and a "good motivator." It was during this time that Chávez became convinced that at some point during his career, military officers would be needed to run the government of Venezuela.

Venezuela was in a political and economic crisis. In the 1970s, oil prices had been high and the Venezuelan economy had seemed strong. Chávez knew from experience that this had not helped most of the poor people in his hometown or others like them, but, as in the 1870s and 1880s, a strong economy made for a secure government. During the 1960s, presidents were elected democratically and, in 1969, for the first time in Venezuelan history, power passed smoothly from one party to the other after an election. Yet many people began to believe that power passed too smoothly and, in fact, was really staying in the same people's hands: the two parties, COPEI and AD, signed the pact of Punto Fijo (named for the place it was signed) in 1958, which said that they would share power and take turns governing. Yet over time, the platforms of the two parties merged and blurred. It seemed to be a one-party system pretending to be a two-party system.

So, people could vote, but voting seemed meaningless if it didn't matter which candidate was elected. Although these governments may genuinely have wanted change, to make people's lives better, they were mired in bureaucracy. Carlos Andrés Pérez of the AD party spent more money between 1974 and 1979 than all Venezuela's previous governments put together, yet so much of the money disappeared through corruption and inefficiency, that he left behind huge debts ($8 billion), inflation, and an unstable economy. It wasn't just that programs for the poor didn't work, but that it was nearly impossible to register a car, get a passport, or even get a phone hooked up. People might have to pay bribes to get a phone line, and even then they often couldn't get a dial tone because the company had 40-year-old, outdated, half-broken equipment. Additionally, in a system where many more people were paid than worked and many saw their jobs as a secure base from which to collect bribes, ordinary people would find themselves in the ludicrous position of having to bribe someone in order to pay their taxes! Yet people had to be able to prove that they had paid their taxes on property, for instance, if they wanted to sell it, so there they were, having to bribe a government employee to take the money that the government badly needed. Venezuelan economist Robert Bottome says there was not a single public service—education, health care, housing, anything—that was working.

But as long as the economy was strong, nothing changed. Oil would fund everything, people believed. That belief was—and still is—built into the culture and the way Venezuelans think about themselves. The country is rich in oil and so, people believe, if only that money was handed around better, surely there would be enough for everyone. As Christian Parenti writes, "The whole culture has been 'Mama State, Papa State, give me oil money.'" That is the voice of children asking for an allowance, not the voice of people creating a working economy. And yet there remained the obvious injustice of some people having had all that oil money, while so many other people suffered.

The stereotype of Venezuelans in the 1970s was of women shopping—in Florida or in Paris—and always saying, "That's so cheap, I'll take two," so that they were called *Dáme dos*, the "give me two" ladies. The unit of currency, called the bolivar, was worth so much that even the most expensive designer clothes in other countries were cheap. Also, imported goods were cheap. Even the very poor people of Venezuela acquired televisions during that time, perhaps as many of 98 percent of people in Caracas—far more than could get telephones.

But by the time Chávez was in the military, the economy was coming apart. The price of oil had fallen and, with it, the value of the bolivar. Most people had less and less money, and people who had been middle class became poor.

In December of 1982, Chávez was unexpectedly ordered to make a speech to 1,200 officers and troops. Without notes, perhaps without having even planned what he was going to say, Chávez began to speak about Latin America's history of oppression. Two-hundred years after its independence from Spain, he said, people were still oppressed. The commander of the military base, Colonel Manrique, hearing about the speech, berated him, saying, "Chávez, you sound like a politician." Captain Felipe Acosta Carles, one of the men who agreed with Chávez, said, "You are wrong, my commander. Chávez is no politician. He is a captain of today's men, and when you hear what he said in his speech, you will piss in your pants." Colonel Manrique told the troops that Chávez had spoken without his permission or knowledge and ordered that none of what Chávez had said was to be spoken of off the base.

Hugo Chávez, Felipe Acosta Carles, Jesús Urdaneta Hernández, and Colonel Rafael Baduel traveled on horseback to Samán del Guëre, six miles away, near Maracay. At the site of a famous tree, where Bolívar is said to have rested, they swore the oath Bolívar had sworn in Rome, in 1805, when he pledged himself to freeing Latin America from Spanish rule. Only a few words had to be changed. The men said, in part: "I swear before you, and I swear before the God of my fathers, that I will not allow my arm to relax, nor my soul to rest, until I break

Although Chávez was transferred from the military academy, he would soon return to Caracas to work in the presidential palace. This photograph shows the contrast between Caracas's downtown skyscrapers and its slum housing.

the chains that oppress us and oppress the people by will of the powerful." (Bolívar had said, "until I break the chains that oppress us by will of Spanish power.")

The men took this oath to bind themselves to a new organization, Revolutionary Bolívarian Movement—200, named for the 200th anniversary of Bolívar's birth. It was started, Richard

Gott said, "more as a political study group than as a subversive conspiracy." Still, from their study of the problems of their country, they began to believe that a coup d'etat, a military overthrow of the government, would be necessary. Venezuela's democracy seemed to them to be failing, as the two parties passed power back and forth. It might as well be a dictatorship, they believed. "Everything has basically remained the same," Chávez said later, in 1999. "It's been the same system of domination" whether the leader rode a horse or drove a Mercedes Benz. Leaders became rich and corrupt; ordinary people, the majority of Venezuelans, still could not "determine their own destiny."

As the movement grew, military intelligence agencies became aware that something was going on, though they probably didn't know how many people were involved. Richard Gott suggested that the military authorities did know that a number of popular and successful young officers were involved and so it would have been difficult to discharge them all from the army. Instead, recognizing Chávez as a likely troublemaker, authorities transferred him in 1986 away from the military academy, where he could influence so many young people, to the far reaches of Venezuela, to Elorza in the state of Apure, close to the border of Colombia. Once there, Chávez was prevented from political organizing, yet he was able to put to the test some of his political theories. In Elorza, Chávez used the military base as a place to experiment with cooperation between the military and civilians, organizing oral history programs and "providing military support for social and economic development in the area." In 1988, the military reassigned Chávez again, this time back to Caracas, to the presidential palace of Miraflores.

# 6

# The 1989 Riots and the 1992 Coup Attempt

ON FEBRUARY 27, 1989, RIOTS BEGAN IN THE STREETS OF GUERENAS, A TOWN 30 kilometers (19 miles) east of Caracas, and then spread to Caracas and nearby towns. The trigger was something that seems small: that morning, people went to get on their regular buses to go to work and discovered that the bus fares had doubled. What began as dismayed grumbling rapidly escalated into a full-scale riot. People flipped over buses and set them on fire, and young people began to pour down the mountains from Caracas's huge barrio into the wealthy city center, smashing store windows, looting from them, and then burning the stores. They looted houses and burned whole city blocks.

The riots, the worst in Venezuela's history, came to be called the *Caracazo*. It might be translated as "the Caracas smash" since the ending *–azo* suggests a "blow." The Caracazo was like a nightmare come true for the richer people who lived and worked in the city.

Caracas was—and is—two cities: one is a sleek, noisy, modern city of glass skyscrapers, expensive stores, fancy malls, and restaurants. The wealthy live on the slopes of Mount Avila in large houses with pools and gardens that are fenced off by walls topped with razor wire and defended by private security guards. On the other side of the mountain are Caribbean beaches. It is an elegant city that fulfilled Guzman Blanco's nineteenth-century dream of a city on par with the great cities of Europe.

The other Caracas is the shanty towns, *barrios,* that have grown up around Caracas on the steep hills that frequently collapse during the rainy season. The houses are shacks made of flattened metal cans, cardboard, canvas, and scraps of wood. They are constructed illegally, yet, since 1958, the government has often allowed people to stay, not knowing where else to put them. Often, after a few years of not having to pay rent, people in the barrios will begin to replace their houses with ones made of brick, but they are without running water or sewers. Some of the houses do have electricity, though, since they are able to illegally tap the electrical lines.

Even before the riots, the well-to-do of Caracas feared the shanty dwellers and imagined them as a kind of subhuman, entirely lawless people. Recently, wealthier people in Caracas told journalist Alma Guilleroprieto, "thieves, murderers, drug addicts, *Chavistas* swarm in those heights." She said the shanty towns looked to her like a lot of places where poor people are coming home from school and parents are taking care of their families and trying to earn a living. It is true, though, that Caracas had become a dangerous city, with a high crime rate. In the riots—as in riots everywhere—all the old pent-up anger came out.

The riots continued for one and a half days, unchecked. As televisions (and remember, nearly every family had a television) showed the rioters, others joined in. When at last the military was called in, it intervened—brutally. People died inside their houses, as bullets came through the walls. Chávez later said, "You know, you send soldiers into the street, scared, with a rifle and 500 bullets, and they fire them all. They spray the streets with bullets, the hills, the poor barrios!" They did, ending the riots at the cost of many lives, including that of Chávez's friend and coconspirator, Felipe Acosta, who Chávez believes was assassinated.

No one knows for certain how many people died in the riots. Official estimates say that about 300 people died, but others have claimed that the government buried bodies in mass graves and that the real number might be in the thousands. When, years later, the government paid out money to the families of those who had been killed, they awarded money to 1,000 families.

The riots came at a time when no one was expecting them—not the government and not Chávez and his revolutionaries. Chávez, in fact, was running a fever and had been ordered home to bed, though he says he was on his way to the university when he saw soldiers running everywhere and realized what was happening.

Why was everyone caught off guard? Why did a bus fare increase, however inconvenient, spark such violence? It goes back to what had been happening in Venezuelan politics and economics since about the time of Chávez's birth—or, in a way, since colonial days. Venezuela's stability had been based on the two-party system and on the high oil prices that ensured that there was lots of money flowing through the economy. But the oil market collapsed. Venezuela had been a founding member of OPEC (the Organization of Petroleum Exporting Countries) in 1960, an organization created to limit the amount of oil for sale at any one time and thus to control its price. Yet Venezuela had been just one of the countries that then failed to abide by OPEC's agreement. It wanted to sell as much oil as possible and did not consider that the prices would fall if there was too much of it. The oil glut made prices plummet in 1979 and then again beginning in 1986. The exchange value of the bolivar fell, and Venezuela found itself heavily in debt.

Heavily armed personnel carriers drive through Caracas, Venezuela, on March 2, 1989, after three days of violent riots left 200 people dead.

In February 1989, Carlos Andrés Pérez of the AD party was in his third week of reelection. In accordance with the constitution of 1960, he had had to wait ten years after the end of his last term to run for the office again. It was a rule meant to keep any one president from having power for too long, crafted by people who had endured too many years of dictatorship. Pérez had been popular in his first term, which had begun in 1973. But when Pérez was reelected, he faced an economy in deep trouble. The average income per person had dropped by more than 75 percent since 1977, and the bolivar was worth about 90 percent less than it had been five years earlier. Store owners had begun to hoard food, knowing that anything they sold would cost more to restock and that if they held on to their stock they could sell it for more money very soon. Even bread, milk, cornmeal, and beans became expensive.

Pérez had campaigned on a platform of promises he couldn't keep. He told people what they wanted to hear—that oil would save them—but only days into his term of office he had to put into effect a series of financial reforms that went against everything he had promised. On February 16, Pérez had announced a series of measures designed to stabilize the economy.

During his first term in office, Pérez had nationalized the iron, steel, and oil industries; subsidized food and oil prices; and "forgiven" (cancelled) $350 million in debts owned to the government by Venezuelan farmers. He supported the bolivar at a high value so that it could always be exchanged at the bank for a high price in dollars. (Ordinarily the worth of a nation's currency fluctuates naturally, but a government can keep the worth of the currency high, although it is very expensive to do so.)

But when Pérez took office for the second time, Venezuela couldn't pay its debts to foreign nations or to the World Bank. In order for Venezuela to get the loans it needed and time to pay off its debts, Pérez had to agree to a series of measures designed to stabilize the economy. These measures went against everything he had done during his first term and everything he had promised for the second, but they were required of him by the IMF (International Monetary Fund) and the World Bank. They included privatizing state companies, removing subsidies (from oil and food, for instance), and letting the bolivar fall in value.

So many Latin American economies faced financial crises in the 1980s that a series of policies called the Washington Consensus were developed to address them. The policies include the ones mentioned above and also lower taxes on people in high income brackets and elimination of regulations that get in the way of economic competition. It emphasizes national and international competition. Although the policy's supporters believe that in the long run it creates a healthy economy, many other people—including Chávez and some economists—believe the policies look out for the interests of big businesses, but not those of the people, especially poor people. Visited upon Venezuela without warning, the policies wreaked havoc.

One part of these measures was that the price of oil—which was always sold extremely cheaply to Venezuelans, subsidized by the government—would double on Sunday, February 26. The government had told the bus companies not to pass on the entire cost of the increase to riders at the same time, but rather to raise fares a little at a time. But the bus companies saw no reason to absorb the cost themselves, so they did double the fares that Monday.

The force of the riots, the violence of the military response, and the shock of upper-class Venezuelans showed that tensions and troubles ran deeper than bus fares, deeper than a disrupted economy. It was also the result of the historical gap between rich and poor, people of color and the white quasiaristocracy. Before the riots, Venezuelan journalist Francisco Toro explained, Venezuelans saw themselves and were seen by others as *the* successful democracy in Latin America: they were different, better, more modern than other countries in the region. They drank the most expensive Scotch whiskey and drove Jaguars. They were *Venezuela Sauditá*, "Saudi Venezuela," rich and modern.

The Caracazo was very much the sort of event that Chávez and his supporters had been waiting for, but they were entirely unprepared to take advantage of it. Compared to the 1958 rebellion in which the "Patriotic Junta" had overthrown dictator General Pérez Jiménez, the 1989 riots were chaotic and leaderless. But the Caracazo riots were, Chávez believes, a response to Washington Consensus programs and to the further betrayal of the poor.

Returning to work at the presidential palace of Miraflores after the Caracazo, Chávez says that the palace guards questioned him about the Bolívarian Movement. "We'd like to know more about it; we're not prepared to go on killing people," he reports their saying. Chávez saw this as a good sign. It was like when he rebelled against the killing of the guerillas. Members of the military were saying that they wanted to do something other than shoot poor people. Although there is no way to verify that this happened, it does show us the development of Chávez's thinking about the role of the military. He wanted them to have a role that didn't involve killing. He wanted them to work on rebuilding the country. Many of Chávez's programs, once he was in power, would involve using the military to work with communities.

On December 6, Chávez and some other officers were accused of plotting a coup or even an assassination of the president and other government officials. Although not convicted, everyone accused was sent far away from the palace. Chávez was sent to Maturin but was allowed to continue his graduate work at Simón Bolívar University in Caracas.

In 1991, Chávez was given the command of a paratrooper battalion based about 80 kilometers (50 miles) from Caracas, in Maracay. From there, Chávez was able to plan the coup, code-named Plan Zamora, after the nineteenth-century general who Chávez so admired. As plans for a coup took shape, Chávez and some of his allies began to disagree among themselves. Guerilla fighter Douglas Bravo, for instance, wanted the coup to begin with civilian action, probably a general strike, with all workers leaving their jobs. (Later, the coup against Chávez began with civilian action.) But Chávez, a member of the military his whole adult life said no, "civilians get in the way. We shall summon them when we get into power."

There were few plans made for what would happen after the coup until very late in the planning. In fact, there was also a lot of disagreement about when the coup would take place. Some

Carlos Andrés Pérez rides in a presidential motorcade in 1989, three years before the bloody coup attempt.

junior commanders said they would launch their own coup if Chávez and his colleagues didn't get moving. But Chávez was told that on February 14, 1992, he would be transferred to a small village near the border of Colombia, so he and the other senior commanders set a date: The plan was coordinated with President Pérez's return from the World Economic Forum in Switzerland on Tuesday, February 4.

Chávez said good-bye to his wife and their children, having made sure she had extra money in the house. Later, when he left his barracks with the soldiers, his last act was to lock the gate behind him and throw away the key. "I realized at that moment that I was saying good-bye to life," Chávez says.

While military forces elsewhere in the country were capturing the barracks at Maracay and other cities, Chávez and five army units marched into Caracas. The units had different tasks. One unit would capture the defense ministry, one would take over Miraflores Palace, and one would go to the airport where Pérez was due to return and take him to the Historical Museum, where Chávez, with his experience in communications equipment, was setting up a base.

Crucially, the forces sent to capture the president failed. Someone had betrayed the conspiracy, and the president was too well guarded to be captured. When Chávez arrived at the museum, he and his troops were fired upon. But (remember the Chávez who talked his way out of Colombia) he was actually able to talk his way out of the situation. He told the colonel who had taken charge of guarding the museum that he and his troops were on their side. However, having gained access to the museum, he discovered that the communications equipment he needed was not there. He had no way to address the Venezuelan people and call for an uprising against the president. (Some sources say that the inability to broadcast recorded tapes to the public took place at a television station.)

The troops trying to take over the palace also failed, and Mrs. Pérez, the president's wife, helped the palace guard defend it.

In other parts of the country, the coup was coming off as planned, and troops took over military barracks and cities including Aragua and Valencia. But without holding the key positions in Caracas or capturing the president, the coup was a failure. On February 4, early in the morning, President Pérez —who, when he escaped capture went not to a fort but to a TV station—announced on television that there had been a rebellion but that it was being put down. At 9:00, Chávez surrendered but persuaded authorities that he be allowed to speak on TV "to avoid bloodshed" and ensure the peaceful surrender of the troops elsewhere. Fourteen soldiers had already died, and 50 soldiers and 80 civilians were wounded. But also, Chávez says now, he wanted to take the initiative, not to turn up later on TV as a defeated-looking captive.

Pérez had told his officers to tape Chávez's words so that they could be edited. But the soldiers didn't want to slow down Chávez's TV appearance and the surrender of the other coup members. They put him on the air live, and as is so often true of Chávez, he found that "an inner voice" rose up in him and the words just spilled out. (To this day, he can repeat the speech word for word.) Chávez said, in part: "Comrades, the objectives we set for ourselves have not been possible to achieve for the moment but new possibilities will arise again, and the country will be able to move forward to a better future. . . . I alone take responsibility for this Bolívarian military uprising."

On the printed page the words don't sound magical, but they made him a hero in under a minute. Richard Gott said it is not only the words, "for the moment" that made an impact. He said that in Venezuela it was unknown for a leader to say that he accepted responsibility for anything or to apologize. In all the years of bank collapses, corruption trials, and misery, no politician had ever apologized or taken responsibility for what they had done or for what had happened on their watch.

Among his coconspirators, Chávez was anything but a hero. He had failed while they had succeeded, and he had, they felt, surrendered much too fast. Why had he given up so fast, coconspirator Commander Urdanta asked him. "I was lonely," he reported Chávez as having replied. Urdaneta pointed out that Chávez, like all the other commanders, had his soldiers and his officers with him. Commander Arias, having asked the same question, got the same reply: "I was left alone, without being able to communicate. . . . I missed you." Jose Ruiz, in whose home a younger Chávez had first read about communism and socialism, refused to visit Chávez in prison. He said: "He should have gone all the way, even if that killed him."

Chávez was sentenced to a long jail term, but he would be pardoned after only two years. The attempted coup, still in the aftermath of the Caracazo, had a deep effect on the political situation. President Pérez would be more blamed than praised for surviving the coup. Ex-president Rafael Caldera made a speech that seemed to support the coup more than it supported the president and his government. Caldera said, noting the lack of popular support for the president, "It is difficult to ask people to sacrifice themselves in a struggle to defend liberty and democracy, when you know that that democracy and the rule of law have not been able to provide them with food . . . [or] to put a stop to the terrible round of corruption that has eroded the institutional legality of the country . . ."

In November 1992, there was another coup attempt, during which the Miraflores Palace was bombed and, in Caracas and Maracay, more than 170 people died in the fighting. This coup failed in part because of another failure in communications and broadcasting: The conspirators took control of a TV station. They were supposed to play a video that would give people the signal to "take to the streets" in protest against the government. But the conspirators played the wrong tape. When the signal came—an air force plane flying over the palace—no one knew what it meant. They had no way of recognizing it as a signal. And, suggested Gott, people could hardly support a coup so disorganized that they couldn't put the right tape in the VCR. It was, again, a political action that hinged on the use of the media and TV.

Although the coups failed, President Pérez was becoming an embarrassment to his own party. He was ousted from power on corruption charges, which may or may not have been trumped up to dispose of him. Certainly, the corruption was real: in one 1989 case, public officials were discovered to have stolen more than $8 billion through a variety of schemes.

Caldera was elected for a second term, on the strength of being anti-Pérez and understanding about people's discontent. Yet neither was he able to fix the economic and social problems of the country. Businesses continued to collapse and

Rafael Caldera walks to the presidential palace after presenting a state of the union address on March 13, 1997. Caldera was president of Venezuela from 1969 to 1974 and from 1994 to 1999, just before Chávez's term.

Venezuelans with money continued to take it and themselves to other countries.

Yares Prison, where Chávez was sent, is not a nice place. "The worst inmates are left to their own devises in two dirty-white, bullet-pocked blocks at the rear of the prison grounds, where black curtains of excrement from broken toilets slide down the walls. . ." reported Jon Lee Anderson in 2001. Many of the prisoners carry guns.

Yet for Chávez, prison was not entirely a bad experience. He had a chair in the open air, protected from other prisoners. He had a plaster bust of Simón Bolívar to talk to, but he was also allowed real visitors to talk to. He was allowed TV and radio interviews. He was treated as an imprisoned military officer, not as a criminal, and he used at least part of the time to plan future rebellions.

Among Chávez's visitors were his wife, Nancy, and their children. Rosa, at age 14, could only cry, he says, but 12-year-old Maria, he says proudly, was glad to see him and full of personal news. She wrote him letters saying that she had some under-standing of her father's political activities: "Now I finally under-stand why you used to arrive home at night worn out, and why you bored us sitting there reading 'A Prayer to Simón Bolívar in the black night of the Americas.'" But also, he says, she told him that she was so proud to be his daughter that she wanted to shout it out on the bus: "I am *comandante* Chávez's daughter!"

This is not to say that prison was fun. "We experienced all the human misery there—we came into direct contact with it," says Chávez. One of its long-term effects is that he developed an eye problem that was not treated properly, leaving him with perma-nent damage to his vision. "But in the end," he told interviewer Aleida Guevara, daughter of revolutionary Che Guevara, "those of us who confronted life in prison consciously, with dignity and integrity, left it strengthened."

In March, 1994, newly elected President Caldera released the coup leaders from prison. Chávez was, by this time, so popular a figure that all the candidates had had to promise to free him. When Chávez was asked at the first press conference, "What are you going to do now?" he replied instantly, "I am going to get into power." He did not know if this was possible.

# 7

# The Election of Chávez

**RELEASED FROM PRISON, CHÁVEZ BEGAN TO REORGANIZE HIS LIFE,** politically and personally. He divorced his wife, Nancy, something he doesn't discuss. He also re-formed the MBR-200 as Movimiento Quinta Republica—MVR. The V is for the Roman numeral 5, as in, the Fifth Republic. Since Venezuela's declaration of independence from Spain in 1811, Venezuela had had four republics.

Soon after leaving prison, Chávez was invited to Cuba, where, in September 1994 he was greeted warmly by Fidel Castro. While the United States has maintained an embargo on Cuba since Castro came into power in 1959, Latin American countries have more often remained on cordial terms with him.

Returning from Cuba, Chávez began to travel around the country, talking to people. He wanted to find out if people would vote for him or if there needed to be another coup—"which would have been crazy," he concluded. He also talked about the

Fidel Castro (right) embraces Hugo Chávez at the University of Havana, Cuba, on December 14, 1994.

idea of a constitutional assembly. He wanted a group of people to rewrite the constitution as a way of reorganizing the government, and he wanted that group to include ordinary people, not just politicians. Rewriting the constitution is how most new governments in Venezuela's history began. Chávez started to believe that there would be real support for him as a presidential candidate. He began to campaign for office.

Toward the end of 1996, while campaigning for office, Chávez met his second wife, the journalist Marisabel Rodríguez. They married in a private ceremony in December of 1997, when their daughter Rosa Inés, named for Chávez's grandmother, was three months old. Marisabel already had a son, Raúl Alfonzo. Critics of Chávez say that Marisabel was the perfect choice for a Venezuelan presidential candidate—a pretty, blond, blue-eyed, light-skinned woman.

Chávez continued to travel widely during the campaign, "crisscrossing the country, meeting with every fire chief and parish priest," wrote the *American Spectator*, sounding somewhat sarcastic about the matter. But his willingness to talk to ordinary people is one of his strengths. "I don't think that we skipped a single city, town, encampment, Indian village, or neighborhood," Chávez says with some pride. He had always been a charismatic speaker, with seemingly limitless energy and vibrancy. His staff (when he became president) says he sleeps very little and consumes a tremendous amount of coffee (in recent years they have cut him down from 26 to 16 cups of espresso a day.) He is tremendously skilled in speaking impromptu—for hours—and making connections to people. And as an obviously mixed-race candidate and one from a poor background, he represents for the majority of Venezuelan people someone who looks like them and speaks like them, who shares their concerns.

Chávez's campaign platform had three main points:

1. The end of *puntofijismo*, the deal between the Christian Democratic Party (COPEI) and the Social Democratic Action Party (AD) that ensured that only their candidates would take turns controlling the presidency.
2. The end of political corruption.
3. The end of poverty in Venezuela.

These were lofty goals, but appealing ones (except to members of COPEI and AD). Estimates say that 80 percent of Venezuelans were still living in poverty, and 33 percent were working for (or at least getting paychecks from) the bloated government bureaucracies. And the corruption was so out of control that one politician who admitted that oil money was illegally flowing into his open pockets came up with this slogan about himself: "He dunks, but he splashes." In other words, I'm stealing lots, but that's OK because I share. In 1998, Transparency International, an international watchdog organization, identified Venezuela as one of the ten most corrupt countries in the world—all of which is worth keeping in mind when Chávez's current opponents bemoan the good old days of pre-Chávez democracy in Venezuela.

Many people watching the campaign found Chávez to be "a mystery man," "a chameleon in a mirror." He spoke of "boiling politicians' heads in oil," but, as the elections grew closer, he suggested that he would be willing to work with the business community. Sometimes he wore his military uniform (which was against military regulations, since he had resigned from the military after leaving prison) and a revolutionary's red beret. At other times he dressed in a conservative shirt and tie. Was Chávez a fiery revolutionary or just another populist candidate who would settle down within the system once elected? No one was sure.

*People* magazine ran a short article on the elections, called "Not Just a Pretty Face." The pretty face in question was not Chávez's but that of one of his main opponents: "Former Miss Universe Irene Saez vies to become Venezuela's first woman president," said the article's subhead. Six months before the election, Saez had about a 22 percent approval rating in the polls, ahead of all but Chávez in a field of 12 candidates. Although *People* said her looks certainly didn't do her any harm in a country that prides itself on its beautiful women and produces Miss Universe beauty pageant winners with some regularity, the writer also noted that she had experience in politics. She was serving her second term as mayor of the richest borough of Caracas and came from a solidly conservative well-to-do background. Her campaign platform issues included better education, smaller government, and law and order. She had won with 96 percent of the vote in her second term as mayor, having cut crime, kept the streets clean, and also outlawing "excessive kissing in the streets."

Ironically, it was COPEI's decision to back Saez that may have led to her loss. The old two-party system was indeed on its last legs, and, not having a candidate of their own, COPEI decided to throw their support behind the candidate that was most clearly one of them (socially and economically) and likely to win. Their support resulted in her approval rating dropping from 22 percent (six months before the election) to 2 percent. COPEI then withdrew its support and announced that it backed Henrique Salas Römer, another conservative candidate. In the election, on December 6, 1998, Chávez won with slightly more that 54 percent of the vote. Salas received only 39 percent. It was the first time a candidate not of the two parties had won. It was the largest majority by which a candidate had won an election in all the 40 years of Venezuelan democracy. Yet at the same time it was a tremendously unpopular election result among people who owned large businesses and among foreign investors. After the election, even more people with money left the country, and foreign investors pulled $1.7 billion out Venezuela. In 1999, 600,000 jobs would be lost.

President Hugo Rafael Chávez Frías took office on February 2, 1999. While still in prison, he had planned to write his thesis about how to turn his Bolívarian movement into a government. Although the thesis was never finished, he now could try his ideas out in real life. He began immediately to try to put into effect his campaign promises. He turned part of the presidential palace into a high school for homeless teens and

Former Miss Universe Irene Saez was unable to beat Chávez in Venezuela's 1998 presidential race.

made corporations pay taxes that hadn't paid taxes in previous years (or ever).

He also started his Plan Bolívar 2000. It was based on his belief that the military can have a variety of roles in national life, some of them having nothing to do with guns. He wanted to use the military to institute social and economic improvement for the poor and in rural regions. Forty-thousand soldiers would help with such things as the building of roads and housing, conducting mass vaccinations, and delivering food. In an interview in 2002, Chávez said, "My order was: 'Go house to house combing the terrain. . . . Who is the enemy? Hunger.' And we started it on February 27, 1999, ten years after the Caracazo, as a way of vindicating the military. . . . Ten years ago we came out to massacre the people, now we are going to fill them with love." One year after the Caracazo, the news magazine *Momento* had run a special issue. Its cover said (in Spanish): "One year after the 27th of February: A thousand deaths and nothing changes." Chávez wanted people to feel that something *had* changed and, given that the price of oil was extremely low ($8 a barrel) when he came to office and the country was deeply in debt, he was in a difficult position.

Chávez had come into office promising a new constitution, which had last been rewritten in 1961. In order to accomplish these things, Chávez called for two national votes.

Chávez asked people to vote on whether they wanted to create a national constitutional assembly, a body that would write the new constitution. The second vote was to elect members of that assembly. The vote on the referendum to rewrite the constitution passed overwhelmingly—71.78 percent to 28.22 percent; however, as with other votes, many people—55.63 percent of the population—abstained, which in Venezuelan history suggests that people protested by not voting. Chávez's party, the MVR, and its allies then received enough votes to give them 120 seats, of 131 total, in the Constitutional Assembly. The assembly also had toll-free telephone lines installed so that ordinary people could call in opinions, and some members of the assembly traveled around the country and organized regional assemblies to discuss the new constitution.

Although formed for the purpose of writing a new constitution, the Constitutional Assembly itself was an independent branch of government. In August 1999, it created a judicial emergency committee able to remove judges from their jobs; it removed 8 of the 15 members of the Supreme Court (on the grounds of corruption). It then declared a legislative emergency and said that the National Assembly, the bicameral (two house) branch of government (like the U.S. Congress), could not meet at all.

In the new constitution, the name of the country was changed to the Bolívarian Republic of Venezuela. It lengthened the presidential term from five years to six years and allowed a president to serve two terms in succession. In what would appear to be a check on greatly enlarged presidential powers, it made a provision for a presidential recall referendum, allowing voters to call for a vote to remove the president from office once they had collected enough signatures on petitions. The new constitution changed the National Assembly from a bicameral legislature to a unicameral one. The new constitution also forbade the privatization of the oil companies owned by the state and extended labor and social security benefits. There were many other changes in the very long document, including a list of the rights of Venezuela's indigenous peoples.

The new constitution, voted into effect in December of 1999, consolidated presidential powers in ways that made Chávez's opponents very nervous. His supporters considered it a constitution that would allow Chávez to carry out his reforms and weed out old, complacent, or even corrupt parts of government. The changes in the constitution, as well as many of Chávez's actions after that (and the behavior of the Constitutional Assembly), led Chávez's critics—within Venezuela and outside, including in the United States—to question whether the process was democratic at all or whether Chávez was gradually turning into a particularly charismatic caudillo ("strong man" dictator) of the sort that Venezuela knows so well.

One of Chávez's political goals is to move people away from the poorest parts of the cities and back to the countryside, to "self-sustaining agro-industrial communities." He wants to "repopulate the countryside." The need to remove some of the shantytowns was made obvious the same day the country voted on the new constitution.

Most of Venezuela doesn't have a cold winter, but it does have a rainy season—as much as 60 to 80 inches (152 to 203 cm) in the llanos and about 33 inches (84 cm) around Caracas. That's only about as much rain as Chicago gets each year, but Caracas gets most of it in one season, within a few weeks. It often causes landslides, but in December of 1999, the Avila Mountain north of Caracas "exploded" as especially heavy rains washed houses, people, and the land itself right off the mountainside. Hundreds of thousands of people lost their homes and stores. Fifteen to twenty thousand died. Chávez took it as a chance to show what the military could do, and people were housed in stadiums, in soccer fields, and in tents near army installations. Chávez, wearing his revolutionary red beret and his camouflage uniform, oversaw the operation.

About 2,000 of the people made homeless eventually agreed to move to one of Chávez's new communities, far from the city. Richard Gott, usually a supporter of Chávez's plans, questioned whether this desire of Chávez to move people out of the cities may be "utopian," in the sense that it is an ideal, but an impossible ideal. The choice, as Gott said Colonel Manrique stated, is this: Do you stay in a familiar place, among friends and neighbors, having trouble making a living and also knowing that your neighborhood will fall down the mountain every 20 years or so, or do you go live in the countryside, with strange bugs and no city, far away from everything familiar and hope that the government actually gives you the land and the job it promised?

The landslide (and an estimated $15 billion price tag to rebuild structures and relocate people) did not make Chávez's first year in office any easier.

Further elections, in July 2000, were held to elect a new National Assembly (Chávez's wife and brother both ran for office and won seats on it) and to reelect Chávez himself under the terms of the new constitution. Although Chávez's critics have claimed that all the elections are rigged and do not

President Hugo Chávez briefs paratroopers on December 18, 1999, before their departure to rescue flood survivors in Venezuela. The natural disaster left more than 200 dead and 7,000 missing.

accurately reflect how people have voted, the elections have all been monitored by the Carter Center, ex-president Jimmy Carter's center for checking the fairness and accuracy of international elections. Only the July elections of 2000 were not validated by the Carter Center, which stated that government pressure and "lack of transparency" made it impossible to say if the election results were valid or not. That this was an exception among Chávez-initiated elections doesn't comfort his opponents much. The question of whether Chávez would use his presidency to unify the country and include and respect the views of people who had not voted for him was beginning to have an answer: No.

Furthermore, on December 3, 2000, Chávez angered the labor unions by backing a law that would require the unions to hold state-monitored elections. That is the sort of interference unions do not want, and Chávez's demand was condemned by international labor groups. (Labor leaders admitted that there was corruption within labor unions, they just didn't want Chávez taking them over.) Finally, Chávez proposed and had the National Assembly pass something called an Enabling Act. Under the provisions of this act, Chávez could rule by decree for a year: he could make laws that did not have to be passed by the congress. (These were intended, said Richard Gott, "to revolutionize the country's infrastructure.") The two previous presidents had asked for and been given similar powers. Before the act expired in November 2001, Chávez enacted 49 decrees. These decrees included provisions for the government to seize and redistribute land, including privately owned land, that was not being used and give it to others. This could include government land or the large country estates of wealthy businessmen.

The basis of Chávez's political and economic moves, including the most radical, is his Bolívarian Revolution. Chávez says that the goals of Bolívarianism, which include his campaign promises, but go further, are

1. Venezuela will have complete sovereignty and not give in to international, imperialistic forces.
2. Popular votes and referenda will assure the political participation of Venezuela's people (hence his helping create a constitution that allows for presidential recalls).
3. Economic self-sufficiency. He wants more of Venezuela's food and consumer goods to be produced within the country.

4. That there will be support for patriotic service.
5. Fair and equitable distribution of Venezuela's oil revenue.
6. Elimination of corruption.
7. Elimination of puntofijismo, the two-party system that excluded members of other parties from the presidency.

Obviously, Chávez's approach to government and economics is the opposite of the Washington Consensus methods of repairing a damaged economy. Its emphasis is on the redistribution of money and resources and on social welfare programs. Even the new constitution is prolabor and makes business owners fear the cost of doing business in Venezuela.

So, there were economic reasons for many people to distrust and dislike Chávez, even before he was elected. They believed (and still believe) that he is bad for democracy, bad for the economy, and bad for international relations with the United States and much of Europe.

There are also reasons that have to do with who Chávez is, socially, racially, and educationally. He does not sound like a president to his critics. They dislike the "folksy" manner—it's the word used over and over again—he uses while speaking on *Alo Presidente*. They don't want a president who rambles on and on, and who sings. When he appeared on his television show holding a flashlight while military doctors performed an operation, he then joked, "You see? Now I can even do surgery!"

The day after that broadcast, some wealthy Venezuelans said, "Did you see our Clown Prince last night?" They don't just think it is sort of silly. They find him really embarrassing—folksy, corny, undignified. They say of him, "The peon [landless peasant] has taken over the farm" (*El péon ha tornado la finca*). Some middle- and upper-class Venezuelans call him *ese mono*—"that monkey." They make a pun of *mi comandante* ("my commander"), instead saying he is *mico mon-*

*dante*—"order-giving monkey." He is to them, says reporter Alma Guillermoprieto, the *zambo*, the "half-breed," "who has empowered other zambos like him to feel at home in their restaurants and beachside resorts. Their restaurants!"

Chávez says, "There is racism here. It used to be more hidden and now it is more open."

And so Chávez is, for many people, an enemy, not only because they dislike his economic and political policies, but because they dislike having a man of mixed blood in the presidential palace. He does not sound like them and he does not look like them. He looks like their servants, like the guy who should be collecting garbage. Many people love him for those same reasons, but since Chávez's response to this has been to call his opponents "rancid oligarchs and squealing pigs" and "the squalid ones," the political divisions in the country grow and grow. And from early on, his opponents have wanted to bring him down.

# 8

# The 2002 Coup d'Etat Attempt

BEFORE THE COUP AGAINST CHÁVEZ IN 2002, HIS POLITICAL OPPONENTS had tried various means to force him out of office.

In 2001, retired general Fernando Ochoa Antich told journalist Jon Lee Anderson, "There is a growing movement within the opposition to unseat Chávez by means that are neither conventional, electoral, nor democratic. The hope is that this situation will not bring about a military coup, that it will be dealt with using constitutional means." He spoke of a situation in which Chávez would resign—although, the general said he couldn't quite imagine how this would come about. Many work stoppages and strikes took place as protests against the president.

By the end of 2001, street vendors in Caracas were selling CDs of the sound of banging pots to people who wanted to drown out and protest their president's long speeches.

On April 9, 2002, Carlos Ortega Carvajal, the leader of Venezuela's largest union federation, Venezuelan Workers Confederation (traditional allies of the AD party), called for a general strike. Fedecameras (the organization of businessmen, historically opponents of the workers' organization), told businesses to close for 48 hours, which is called a lockout. Usually, a strike is workers against management, and a lockout is management against workers. In this instance, the two sides united against the president, believing that his policies were bad for them all.

On April 11, somewhere between 500,000 and 1,000,000 people turned out for a demonstration—a protest march—that would march to the headquarters of PDVSA, Venezuela's state-owned oil company. Only a few days earlier, Chávez had fired the seven-person management board of the company, on television, by blowing his baseball umpire's whistle and shouting "You're out!" After Ortega addressed the marchers at PDVSA headquarters, he told them to march to the presidential palace. For many of the protesters, this must have been an unexpected detour, but the leaders of the workers, business owners, and media had already agreed that this strike was for the purpose of forcing the president out of office. For several days before the strike, the four main private TV stations had played hours of anti-Chávez speeches, calling for people to march in the streets and demand the president's resignation.

What happened at this time is hotly debated, notwithstanding the fact that events were actually being recorded live on video. A group of Irish filmmakers, who were in the palace to film Chávez, found themselves in the unusual position of filming a coup in progress.

At the presidential palace, about 5,000 Chávez supporters had gathered. When the opposition protesters arrived, the two groups began to throw stones and tear gas at each other. Then shots were fired, from both sides. One journalist who was present, Gary Wilpert, said, "I saw clearly that there were three parties involved in the shooting: the city police [anti-Chávez], Chávez supporters,

Supporters of ousted president Hugo Chávez burn tires in the streets of Caracas on April 13, 2002.

and snipers from buildings above." It was impossible, he says, to figure out who fired the first shots. Also, Wilpert does not account for the actions of the National Guard, who were pro-Chávez.

In the end, about 20 people were killed and more than 100 were wounded, on both sides. Coup leaders blamed Chávez for the deaths and said that these "murders" were reason enough to remove him from office.

While bullets flew, Chávez commandeered the TV stations, both public and private, an event common enough in Latin

America that it has a name—*cadena*—which is to say, it's not something he invented, to ask people to go home. Private stations ignored (or half ignored) the cadena: they split the screen between Chávez and the broadcasts of the uprising (or their version of it). Their version of what was happening showed Chávez supporters shooting unarmed people from an overpass; this was contradicted by the footage shot by the Irish filmmakers.

A number of senior military officers went on television calling for the president to resign, and naval officer Vice Admiral Hector Ramirez Perez went on the air saying, "The President of the Republic has betrayed the trust of the people, he is massacring innocent people with snipers."

When Chávez tried to call on the military to surround Miraflores Palace and protect him, he found that the exits from nearby military bases had been blocked and that the generals had been told to arrest him. Some of the National Guard and the air force had also joined the coup.

Early in the morning of April 12, General-in-Chief Lucas Rincón Romero appeared on television and said that Chávez had been asked to resign as president and had done so. Chávez said later that he had agreed to resign—*if* that was truly the will of the people and if certain conditions were met. He said the constitution had to be respected, that the National Assembly had to be notified, that his vice president would be allowed to succeed him, that everyone in the palace and his family be safe, and that he be allowed to take sanctuary in Cuba. But, he says, when the news channels announced his resignation, he had not resigned, and as he was told that his demands were unacceptable, he would not resign. He was then arrested, supposedly for the deaths of the protestors, and taken to Fort Tiuna. He expected to be killed.

That morning, Chávez discovered that some of the soldiers guarding him were still loyal to him, and he asked them for a television and a cell phone. The news programs said over and over again that he had resigned, even though he hadn't. They said the military was entirely in favor of the coup. Chávez knew

## THE NEWS PROGRAMS SAID OVER AND OVER AGAIN THAT HUGO CHÁVEZ HAD RESIGNED, EVEN THOUGH HE HADN'T.

that wasn't true from calls he had made the night before. And, appearing on the bottom of every television screen were the words, "Chávez resigned; democracy restored."

Chávez was able to reach two people by phone whom he knew he could trust—his wife and his elder daughter. His wife, Marisabel, called the U.S. news station CNN, and daughter Maria Gabriela reached Fidel Castro, and told them what had happened. And so, a coup that was supported by and in part created by Venezuelan television was denounced and undone, in part, by the TV station CNN and by Radio Havana, both of which said that Chávez had in fact not resigned. But that news would not be broadcast on Venezuelan television for another day, although at least one station, Radio Caracas Television (RCTV), had been told that Chávez had been kidnapped.

In the meantime, two representatives from the military legal department visited Chávez to report on his health. Since this was being treated as a resignation, there were legal formalities to be conducted. But when the representatives left Chávez, one carried with her a message on the bottom of a form: "He said that he had not resigned." The chief legal officer of the government, Isais Rodríguez, received the message by fax and then announced it on television, but the coup wasn't over yet.

People watching television also saw Fedecameras leader Pedro Carmona sworn in as interim president. Carmona then began immediately to dismantle the government. He removed "Bolívarian" from the country's name, dissolved the National Assembly (promising new elections for a bicameral assembly within a year), repealed the 49 laws that gave the government greater control of the economy, reinstated the old heads of

Petroleas de Venezuela (the ones Chávez had fired), and dismissed the Supreme Court (and other) judges. He also suspended the constitution.

Carmona made a number of errors. He failed to give Carlos Ortega, who had helped engineer the coup, a role in the new government. Worse—from the standpoint of creating a stable situation—Carmona began to dismantle the high command of the armed forces. He wanted to eliminate Chávez's old supporters in the military, but he also dismissed General Vázquez Velasco, who had helped carry out the coup. He thus insulted and alienated people who had helped him and whose help he still needed very badly.

Chávez had seemed too far to the left and not democratic enough to many people, but he had at least been elected. Carmona, coming into power through a coup (or, he claimed, a "power vacuum"), not through an election, was immediately showing himself to be more authoritarian, no more democratic, and too far to the right. He had dissolved the government except for himself; he was acting like a dictator. The uprising of pro-Chávez forces, including the presidential guard, began even before the news was broadcast that Chávez had not resigned. But the news got out anyway: although Venezuela's telephone system still didn't work very well, people's cell phones worked just fine, and by April 13, about 100,000 Chávez supporters had taken to the streets around the palace.

Of foreign governments in the Western Hemisphere, only the United States and El Salvador had recognized the new government. That is not the only reason why Chávez would claim (and still claims) that the United States had a role in the coup. It was clear that the U.S. government welcomed it. Otto Reich, a former U.S. ambassador to Venezuela, called a meeting at his Washington, D.C., office and told ambassadors from Latin America and the Caribbean that the coup was not a threat to democracy and that it was, rather, Chávez's antidemocratic behavior that was the threat. Later, evidence would show that Washington knew a week

Businessman Pedro Carmona was sworn in as interim president—for a day—during the failed coup against Hugo Chávez.

ahead of time of the coup. Also, the United States has funded anti-Chávez organizations, at the time of the coup, and since then.

Other Latin American governments—not all of them famous for their respect for the democratic process—refused to recognize the new government. As one Mexican newspaper said, "If this uprising in Caracas had been tolerated, it wouldn't be long before this could have blown up in the face of other democracies."

The coup ended on April 13, just two days after it had begun. Chávez was still at the military base in Turiamo. The soldier who brought him breakfast told him that Commander Baduel of the parachute regiment at Maracay (where Chávez had once been stationed) was refusing to take orders from Carmona's government. But a plan to free Chávez was foiled when the coup supporters moved him to the small offshore island of La Orchila.

Carmona planned to meet with media leaders, who were coup supporters, but when the media arrived at Miraflores they found the palace surrounded by Chavistas, Chávez supporters. News that parts of the military were refusing to accept the new government was getting around. The poor who lived in the hills around the center of Caracas were streaming into the city. The commander of the president's honor guard, Colonel Morao, and the guard retook the palace, showing that the soldiers guarding Carmona were not in fact loyal to him. And he was obliged to flee. He was arrested later that day. At a meeting held by General Vázquez Velasco, officers questioned whether Chávez had in fact resigned—and they objected, anyway, to the dismantling of the government, which they had not been warned about and had not agreed to. So, even some officers who might otherwise have supported a new government refused to accept Carmona and his policies. His behavior in office made many people believe that what had happened was not, in fact, a popular uprising but rather a coup d'etat begun by business interests, including those who owned the TV stations.

Chávez was returned to Miraflores at 3:45 A.M., Sunday, April 14. It was the shortest coup in Venezuelan history. Supporters banged pots and pans in the streets to welcome Chávez back. The president of the stock exchange told a reporter that in the wealthier parts of the city, "It was like the bogeyman had come back. People were crying in church."

For some Venezuelans, the attempted coup, like the riot in 1989, was a wake-up call. The wife of a wealthy businessman told *New York Times* reporter Deborah Sontag, "In the last 20 to 30 years, the private leadership of the country fell in love with the ease of accumulating wealth. . . . We have neglected our society's institutions and let them get corrupt. I know I sound like Chávez, but his arguments about what is wrong with our country are the same as mine. His solutions are back to the Stone Age. . . But his diagnosis is correct." Another woman told a colonel of the presidential guard, "I wasn't a Chavista before the coup, but when I contemplated a dictatorship of the oligarchy, I remembered why we elected Chávez in the first place."

Two weeks after the coup, Chávez appeared on *Alo Presidente*, with the portrait of Jesus to his right, and that of Simón Bolívar to his left, and delivered an unscripted three-hour address on subjects that ranged from details of what had happened when he was deposed to details about the kinds of trees on his patio. Usually quick to spot plots and make accusations (which he would also do, eventually), in this telecast he instead emphasized that he was a good Christian who forgave his enemies and—far from being a caudillo—was perfectly willing to have the country call a referendum in 2003 as allowed by the constitution and then, democratically, vote him out of office if they wanted. "Those who don't want Hugo Chávez to be president of the republic—fine, go organize yourself."

In the wake of the attempted coup, Chávez fired and replaced generals who had not been loyal to him. The Venezuelan Supreme Court ruled in 2002 that the events in April had been a "power vacuum" rather than a coup d'etat, and it dismissed charges against four military officers. They went free amidst public protests. Chávez accepted the court's ruling but would later pursue Ortega for his role in the coup. And in 2004, the Supreme Court ruled that the hearing had been invalid, so it is possible that the officers will face charges.

The coup further divided the Venezuelan people. Some became loyal to Chávez after the coup, preferring an elected, though left-wing, leader to the alternative that presented itself, but by and large, Chávez's opponents remained his opponents. Efforts to remove him from the presidency would continue.

The coup also shook up Chávez's private life. Two months after the coup, in June of 2002, his wife left him. The divorce became final in January of 2004, and she was awarded custody of their six-year-old daughter, Rosa Inés. Marisabel Rodríguez had served on the National Assembly and worked on many programs, nationally and internationally, that sought to protect the rights and safety of children. She did more than most president's first ladies, but she had found being married to this particular president a considerable strain. She had been hospitalized for stress after his election in 1998 and had had to flee the presidential palace with the children. She said, "I can't carry on subjecting the children to the stress of living in a place where we've had to run away three times, practically with our possessions tied in a bundle and hanging from a stick. That's no life for anyone."

Friends of Chávez say he is not a good "communicator" either with his wife or with his children. Weeks before the coup, Marisabel had been interviewed by a magazine and had spoken about how difficult she found her life in the palace. She had wanted to marry the man, she said, and to raise their daughter and her son together; she hadn't realized she was marrying the Bolívarian Revolution. The cover of the magazine had shown her weeping. They had little left in common but their daughter, she said.

## GENERAL STRIKE

Beginning on December 2, 2002, PDVSA workers went on strike. Although the petroleum company had been nationalized 25 years earlier, most of the profits had continued to go to a relatively small group of people.

The strike (by workers) and the lock out (by owners) was historically unusual—a coming together of oil workers, union members, and Fedecameras members (owners) who shut down Venezuela's oil industry for two months. The action—an economic coup rather than a political one—was intended to force Chávez's resignation by shutting down Venezuela's economy. The slogan of the shutdown was "a Christmas without Chávez."

The strike created a great deal of hardship for Venezuela's people. Not only was gas in such short supply that the country had to import it (and there were still long lines at gas stations), but there were power failures and interruptions of public transportation services. Food was became scarce. Chávez says of that time, "the Venezuelan establishment and their international allies sabotaged

The Venezuelan Workers Confederation, led by Carlos Ortega (above), agreed to a strike in April 2002 to protest President Chávez's administration.

the oil refineries, threw away millions of liters of milk and slaugh-tered cattle so there would be no food." Chávez and his supporters called it the "oil terror" instead of the "oil strike." He bought milk, meat, and gas from Colombia and accepted a whole ship full of beans from Cuba. ("Pay whenever you can," he reports Castro as saying.)

In early January 2003, when the strike had already been going on longer than anyone had imagined was possible, Chávez called in the military to guard ports and oil pipelines. The military also kept schools and banks open. He then fired the oil company's directors and appointed a new minister of oil. Eventually 18,000 people working for the oil industry (out of about 40,000) would lose their jobs. After 63 days, the strike ended as a victory for Chávez. He was in control of the oil industry and had eliminated both unnecessary workers and personal opponents.

Like most of Chávez's actions, this one would be controver-sial. The courts said that the firings weren't legal. People who lost their jobs could not get new ones and so many skilled workers left the country. But the United States had not come to the support of the oil industry. The United States had been less supportive of the oil industry shutdown than the coup because by then it had invaded Iraq. The country's attention was on that war, and a Venezuelan oil shutdown simply meant that an important source of oil for the United States became unavailable.

The implications for Venezuela were more complex. The economy took a severe blow. When people—in and out of the country—spoke or wrote in 2003 of Chávez's failures to improve people's lives and end poverty, they tend not to take into account the effects on the economy of over two months of complete eco-nomic disruption.

# 9

# Missions and Oppositions

ONE OF THE OUTCOMES OF THE STRIKE THAT THE STRIKERS HADN'T foreseen was the government takeover of the oil industry. With the industry's billions of dollars per year now available to the government, Chávez was able to greatly enlarge his programs for the poor. The nationwide programs, called *misións*, involve (among other things) health, education, job training, and sub-sidized food.

These include Misión Barrio Adentro; 8,000 Cuban doctors were brought in—the number would later go up to 13,000—to bring medical care, including dental and eye care, to cities and towns. Cuba provided doctors to Venezuela in exchange for cheap oil. (As part of that same agreement, Cuba also sent thousands of sports instructors and teachers.)

Misión Robinson, begun in 2003, was named for Simón Rodriguez, Simón Bolívar's tutor, mentor, and friend, who called himself Samuel Robinson, in honor of the fictional character

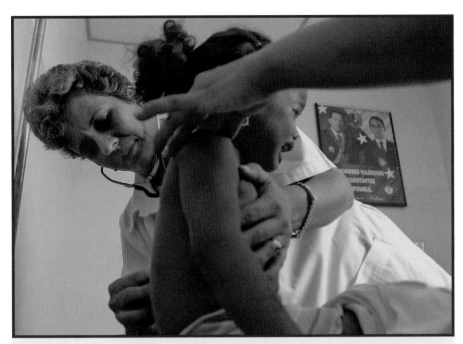

A Cuban doctor examines a child in a medical center in the shantytown of Resplandor in Caracas on July 15, 2003. The medical center is part of Chávez's Misión Barrio program.

Robinson Crusoe. (In the novel, the character lived for 28 years on an island in the Venezuelan river of Orinoco. Crusoe was resourceful and creative and very good at figuring out how to do things than no one had taught him to do.) Misión Robinson provides education—literacy skills and arithmetic—for adults. It isn't just a program that offers people classes, but it includes television programs—also the televisions, although many Venezuelans have those—reading glasses, and materials translated into many indigenous languages. An estimated 1.5 million adults were illiterate when Chávez was elected.

Another literacy program serves high school dropouts. In 2004, for instance, about 600,000 students began a two-year program in which they are paid a small amount of money to help them support themselves while they take courses at night in subjects like math, geography, grammar, and foreign languages.

Other misións prepare high school graduates for university, help unemployed people find jobs, and provide subsidized food and housing. Additionally, there are misións that give land to the poor and to indigenous communities.

Chávez's opponents raise the objection that he is bypassing existing government departments and creating a welfare state in which people will learn to expect everything to be handed to them, for free. They also argue that he is buying votes by buying the love and loyalty of the poor.

Certainly, some of the misións function to provide him with loyal voters. Misión Identidad, begun in 2004, helps people register to vote, including the many people who do not have proper papers—a common problem among poor people, who are less likely to have been born in a hospital or to have their births recorded by the state. The program also helps immigrants from Europe and other Latin American countries to register.

And it is true that Chávez bypasses other systems for his misións, sometimes for efficiency, because the older systems were bloated and moribund—this is the country where citizens had had to bribe tax collectors in order to be able to pay their taxes and to bribe phone company employees to have any chance of getting a phone. At other times, Chávez may be avoiding using existing systems because he wishes to annoy opponents. Misión Mercal, for instance, builds and operates alternative supermarkets, creating a source of cheap, good-quality, government-subsidized food. Misión Mercal doesn't have to pay import duties and so can provide high-quality Uruguayan and Argentinean beef very cheaply. This serves both to provide food (including rice, beans, and other staples) to people who need it at a price they can afford and as a slap at Venezuela's cattle ranchers who have not been among Chávez's supporters. One of his opponents who said, "The poor may

love Chávez, but they don't eat any better," is wrong. The ben-
eficiaries of Misión Mercal not only eat better but also are very
proud of being able to buy good-quality food.

The misións provide things that people need to the very
people whose needs have historically been ignored in Venezuela.
They mean that more people can get to computers (provided
in free computer centers) and fill out job applications, and that
women who work outside the home have access to daycare for
their children. People in need of life-saving medical care have
access to it—easy access, because one of the goals of the medical
misións is to establish community and local medical care, so that
people who are sick or elderly do not have to travel long distances
to get help.

And so the misións have indeed helped create Chávez supporters. When reporter Alma Guillermoprieto spoke to people
helped by the misións, she found people who had been given
hope for the first time. Chávez is sometimes criticized for being a
dreamer. Whether the misións are sustainable—they are currently
funded by the huge oil surplus and if that went away, so would the
misións—is a big question, but how the misións have been imple-
mented shows both Chávez's strengths and weaknesses as a leader.
He has allowed himself to use them to annoy people he dislikes,
the ranchers, for instance. Venezuelan doctors also complain that
Chávez is funding the Cuban doctors but not supporting existing
clinics or facilities. Yet, he has succeeded in getting help to at least
some of the places where it is most needed.

When Guillermoprieto visited a small group of women at a
sort of improvised misión headquarters in an empananda stand
in a poor neighborhood in Caracas, the women had charts of all
the locally available misións and of what was provided by them.
One of the problems of setting up new social programs is making
sure that people—including people who are illiterate or don't trust
the government—know what kind of help is available and how to
get it. Local headquarters work. But when Guillermoprieto asked
a woman at a medical program what she liked best about Chávez

and his missions, the answer wasn't about the programs: "I'm just in love with him. . . He's gorgeous," the woman said.

It doesn't hurt a politician to be loved by the voters, but many people who follow Chávez's career believe that too much of his appeal has been personal charm and his claim to want to help everyone, or at least everyone poor. Chávez has always encouraged people to speak to him personally, to pass him slips of paper asking for help. This means that individuals—poor farmers who are not being paid properly for their work, illegal immigrants, parents who are concerned about a child's schooling—are sometimes offered the president's personal help with their problems. The result is that people travel for days to wait outside the palace to speak with him, to press pieces of paper with requests into his hand, and then assistants try to keep up with the requests. There are long lines of people waiting to see him and rooms of scraps of paper. People who don't catch his eye or happen to come at a bad time may not have their requests heard, no matter how important or justified their request. Chávez likes the idea of people being able to come to him directly, yet it's a questionable way to run a country, making everything dependent on chance and how the president is feeling that day. It makes the government too much about *him*. Having people bring him requests resembles the tradition of people's pinning prayers or requests to a shrine or a statue in church—which is, of course, a tradition familiar and comfortable to many of the Catholics of Venezuela. It is related to his bypassing existing systems—like hospitals—to put his own health-care systems in place. That style of governing both reflects and encourages the belief that everything that came before Chávez was corrupt or useless and that everything good comes directly from him.

## RECALL

In August of 2004, the opposition to Chávez again attempted to remove him from power, this time by constitutional means.

Caracas residents wait in line to vote in the recall referendum on the rule of Chávez on August 15, 2004.

Chávez had built into the 1999 constitution a presidential recall provision; if the signatures of 20 percent of voters could be collected on petitions, then a binding vote had to be held to decide if the president should or should not remain in office.

The collection of signatures began in early to mid-2003, and by August, over 3 million signatures had been collected. When the National Electoral Council (CNE) rejected the first lists, claiming that many were invalid, another signature drive produced 3.6 million signatures by the end of the year.

On August 15, 2004, the recall referendum was defeated, 59 percent to 41 percent, keeping Chávez in office until the end of his term. A significant number of voters—30 percent of those registered—abstained, but the vote was overseen and certified by both the Carter Center and the Organization of American States. Nevertheless, the opposition—which had insisted on the presence of these outside agencies to guarantee fairness—disputed the vote, which polls had told them they would win.

Chávez did not use his victory to try to heal the ever-growing breach between Chavistas and non-Chavistas. He seems to thrive on the polarization of there being Good Guys and Bad Guys. He uses criticism from his opponents—in Venezuela or in other countries—to consolidate his power, even when the vote shows that he has a majority of people supporting him and he could afford to be more generous to his opponents and to listen to their concerns.

Venezuelans who signed the petition calling for the recall vote found themselves on a list—called simply The List, *La Lista*—which was and perhaps still is referred to when people apply for jobs or help from any of the misións. Thus, citizens are being harmed for having used a right granted to them by their constitution. This obviously worries people who are concerned with Chávez's use of his power. People working for Súmate, a group that worked to collect signatures for the recall referendum, are being accused of conspiracy to "destroy the Republican form of government," and face the possibility of 8 to 16 years in jail. The accusation is based on Súmate's having accepted a relatively small amount of money from the U.S. National Endowment for Democracy.

Additionally, in March 2005, the Chávez government passed laws regulating the media. Defenders of Chávez had, earlier, pointed out that his government remained liberal about its critics. But as of March 2005, "disrespect" of public officials on TV and in newspapers or magazines became a criminal offense carrying prison sentences of up to 40 months. Although these new laws have not been enforced regularly, they constitute a chipping away of freedoms and further, and perhaps unnecessarily, hamper the political opposition's effectiveness. (For the last few years, the opposition has been so ineffective that Chávez probably doesn't need to take away their freedoms to stay in power.)

The habit of going out of his way to annoy his opponents and polarize issues is evident in Chávez's international as well as domestic discourse. Since the coup of 2002 and the recall referendum, Chávez has often accused the United States administration of plotting coups or assassinations, claiming to have spotted ships or planes off the coast. That the administration of George W. Bush knew about the coup before it happened and later gave moral support and money to Venezuelan groups involved in the recall referendum only makes Chávez's other claims easier to believe. When Pat Robertson, a high-profile TV evangelist with ties to the White House, called for Chávez's assassination, Chávez was presumably delighted. By vilifying American policies and the American government, he strengthens his position as the good guy. He presents himself as the leader who is looking out for Venezuelan and Latin American economic and cultural interests in a world in which multinational corporations seek to homogenize the world and create a planet of consumers for their products, while ensuring a plentiful supply of oil (from Venezuela and the Middle East) and cheap labor (in China, India, and other parts of the developing world). Chávez has worked with Cuba's Fidel Castro, China's Hu Jintao, and Iran's Mahmoud Ahmadinejad to craft trade agreements favorable to one another but not to the United States or Europe.

Chávez seeks to create an alternative to Western capitalism and to existing international organizations such as NATO. In March of 2005, Chávez said that the FTAA (Free Trade Act of the Americas) was "dead" and that neoliberalist economics had failed in Latin America (which is what some U.S. news programs said the day that Bolivia elected a left-wing, Indian president). Chávez spoke harshly to the Mexican president, Vincente Fox, in November 2005: "The president of a people like the Mexicans lets himself become a puppy in the eyes of the empire." And when Fox protested and threatened to recall the Mexican ambassador to Venezuela if Chávez didn't apologize,

In 2005, Mexican president Vincente Fox agreed with Hugo Chávez to pull their respective ambassadors. Fox and Chávez engaged in a verbal fight, with Chávez threatening, "Don't mess with me."

Chávez instead recalled Venezuela's ambassador to Mexico. He can be—but is not always—quick-tempered and proud.

Chávez wants to create economic and social plans that emphasize Venezuela's Latin American identity. Even before the mudslides of 1999 that left 15,000 to 20,000 people dead and about 100,000 homeless, Chávez—like other Venezuelan leaders before him—had spoken of the need to move some of the urban population of the country, away from the cities and back to the largely uninhabited land. Chávez spoke of his desire for Venezuela to produce more of its own food and for its people to leave the poor barrios of the cities to farm. It's an interesting and complicated suggestion: what does it mean to, in his words, "decentraliz[e] the country and create 'reverse migration,'" which is the opposite of what has happened in developed and developing countries for many decades? "Of course it's not easy," he says. "You can't just arrive at a *barrio* and tell people they've got to decamp to the south, and then leave them to get on with it and survive as best they may."

Chávez is calling for something more than just an attempt to get people out of poor neighborhoods, especially poor neighborhoods that collapse in mudslides in the rainy season. He says he doesn't want children to have to leave home to get an education as he did. He also wants a more "endogenous" future, in which people would produce more of what they consume, especially the traditional products and dietary mainstays of the country, including rice and corn. But this requires changing the eating habits of Venezuelans, who currently eat more than five times as much wheat (which must be imported from the United States) than rice. Chávez, and others who support this goal, envision Venezuelans who will eat "mangoes instead of apples, *arepas* [made of corn] instead of hamburgers, and rice instead of pasta."

Even Richard Gott, who believes very strongly in Chávez and his Bolívarian Revolution, sounded dubious when he reported this. Observing one of Caracas's huge modern shopping malls, he describes Venezuelans enjoying the products of McDonald's, Dunkin' Donuts, Wendy's, and other international fast-food companies. Arepas are likely to be a hard sell to that crowd. Eating habits do change, but eating is one area of life in which it is notoriously hard to *force* change, as various international aid agencies have found historically when they discovered that the people they wanted to help would starve to death rather than eat unfamiliar foods.

Similarly, Chávez says that Venezuela should manufacture toys that reflect the region's history. He suggests, for example, that children play with Simón Bolívar dolls rather than with Barbies or Superman action figures. During the Christmas 2005 season, there weren't many Simón Bolívar dolls to be found in Caracas stores, but 18-inch Hugo Chávez dolls were extremely popular among adults. Pull a string and it says "It's your dream, it's your hope, and it's your job to be free and equal" and "I arrived here to do all that is humanly possible to help all the Venezuelan people." The dolls were made in China, not Venezuela, and were often bought as joke presents for Chávez haters.

Chávez's wish to support Latin American interests and culture is not unreasonable. Many national, religious, and cultural groups worry about the destruction of their native cultures. Historically, there is often a swing back and forth between a country's interest in becoming modern and keeping up with what's happening in the rest of the world, and its concern that it will then lose its own individual identity. In the late 1800s, Guzmán Blanco tried to make Caracas look like Paris, and now Hugo Chávez worries that in valuing what is (North) American and European, Venezuela has forgotten its own indigenous roots. He is asking parts of an urban population to return to the land and ways of their ancestors, who were poor and discriminated against in the first place. He has created Telesur, a South American satellite TV station, to give people an alternative to RCTV's *¿Quien Quiere Ser Millionario? (Who Wants to Be a Millionaire?)*. Telesur offers, instead, a Colombian Indian woman in native dress presenting the news. And, of course, Chávez offers *Aló Presidente*. It really works for some people and it really doesn't for others.

# 10

# The Future of Hugo Chávez

**A PSYCHIATRIST IN CARACAS, DR. PEDRO DELGADO, SAID CHÁVEZ IS GREAT** for his business because Chávez is making people crazy. He doesn't mean it as a joke. He's seeing "anxiety, depression, uncertainty, [and] rage" in his patients. In 2002, interviewed by the *New York Times Magazine* shortly after the coup, he said, "Chávez was an experiment for a society looking for a way out of the old, corrupt order of things. . . . [H]is ambitions were grandiose," that is, unrealistically grand.

Chávez was elected when the old political parties were so out of touch with the electorate that they didn't have a candidate and didn't realize that their endorsement would actually hurt a candidate. The country was in total disrepair financially, so that people with money were already leaving it. Much of the middle class had fallen below the poverty line. Bureaucracy and corruption had brought most agencies, including even the phone company, almost to a standstill. The national currency was in a tailspin, on

Venezuela's economic crisis has proved to be Hugo Chávez's greatest challenge as president. This poverty-stricken neighborhood in Caracas boasts a McDonald's, a favorite of the Venezuelan people, despite Chávez's urge for boycotts.

its way to being worth nothing. And so a broken country elected someone who seemed to offer hope and certainly seemed to offer change. Dr. Delgado said, "We [Venezuelans] have a hard time resisting strongmen who say they will solve all our problems. We want to believe in them, passionately, blindly." And, wrote Tim McGirk, the year Chávez was elected, "Chávez represents a populist backlash against Venezuela's entrenched power elite, whose corruption and ineptitude had virtually bankrupted the oil-rich Caribbean nation."

How is Chávez doing as a leader? By now, it is obvious that the answer depends on whom you ask. Politicians, news stations, journalists, Web sites, historians, or ordinary people—

President Chávez speaks at the inauguration of the new military academic year on January 10, 2006. Defense Minister Orlando Maniglia is seated next to Chávez. The president urged his military to prepare for a war with the United States.

almost all must be identified as primarily pro- or anti-Chávez before their views can be considered. There is not a statistic on unemployment, oil exports, average income, or anything else that could be cited definitively, that someone on one side of the debate or the other would not say is biased and incorrect. A discussion of Hugo Chávez's life and presidency causes us to examine the way we interpret historical events. Was the coup against Chávez an effort to restore democracy or a blow to democracy? When Chávez creates laws to control the media, is that an attempt to limit free speech or could it also be a response to organizations that helped to overthrow the government? Is what Venezuela has now a democracy? Is Chávez on his way to being a dictator?

Hugo Chávez made three campaign promises when he first ran for office: to end the closed two-party system, to end corruption, and to end poverty. How is he doing?

The two-party system is certainly dead for now. Arguably, it was dead even as Chávez campaigned.

Chávez has found corruption intractable. It is socked in like a bad weather system and—even exercising his considerable power—he knows it is bigger than he is. "It is like a cancer that has metastasized in all directions," he says, not just in Venezuela, but in Latin America.

Chávez is certainly trying to end poverty, insofar as he is creating his many programs to help the poor. Yet there is (no surprise) widespread disagreement about how well he is doing. When people examine the figures for poverty and unemployment during the years of the Chávez presidency, they often note that the figures didn't get any better, at least during his early years in office. While opponents blame that on him, they tend to leave out that he inherited a terribly damaged economy that was further debilitated by the severe landslides of 2000 and by the oil strike of 2002–2003. The same people who shut down the economy for slightly over two months then turn to Chávez and say (in effect), See how bad for the economy you are?

Venezuela's National Institute of Statistics says that the poverty level dropped to 35 percent in 2005, (down 8 percent) and that the critical poverty level—"the level at which people cannot afford to cover even basic needs"—dropped 10 percent in the first half of 2005, to 8 percent. Chávez and his misións have given many people hope. Some are getting basic services (like medical care) for the first time. Some are getting jobs for the first time.

But many economists believe that—at best—"Chávez is pursuing good intentions with bad management." His misións would not survive a drop in the price of oil and, historically, oil prices do go up and down. In many ways, he is continuing Venezuela's old policies of depending on one "crop" for its economy, the crop having been oil for many years now.

Additionally, Chávez does not seem to look at the economic big picture. He cannot build a stable economy without

Venezuelan diplomat Jenny Figueredo is embraced by President Chávez at the Miraflores Presidential Palace in Caracas on February 10, 2006. According to Chávez, Figueredo was thrown out of Washington in retaliation for the expulsion of a U.S. official accused of spying on the Chávez government.

some of the people who oppose him, because they are the people who create jobs and generate money for the economy, aside from oil revenue. Among the "elite" of Venezuela are the people who say, "Chávez did something important for this country . . . . He woke us up. After years and years. We have no choice but to embrace our responsibility." But there is no evidence that Chávez is aware of those people or interested in working with them. Far less is he interested in working with the people who truly and completely oppose him, even though those people may be needed to build a new and healthier Venezuela. He would rather give or loan people money to begin their own new businesses. It is indeed a revolutionary stance, as he says.

Although the Venezuelan constitution says that Chávez can be elected for only one more term, to be voted on in December 2006, he says he plans to be in office until 2023. The question remains whether he will survive as president if he continues to polarize the country, and if he does survive, will it be by continuing to consolidate his power and, backed by the military, indeed become the dictator that many people fear? Or is he part of the new wave of Latin American leaders, now joined by the new president of Bolivia, Evo Morales, that country's first Indian president, who are creating a new kind of democracy and serving the needs of the majority of the people in their countries? It remains to be seen.

# CHRONOLOGY

| | |
|---|---|
| **1498** | Christopher Columbus lands in what is now Venezuela. |
| **1783** | Simón Bolívar is born in Caracas. |
| **1811** | Venezuela is declares independence from Spain. |
| **1819** | Bolívar becomes president of *Gran Columbia*. |
| **1823** | The last troops loyal to Spain are defeated and expelled from Venezuela. |
| **1829** | Venezuela breaks away from *Gran Columbia*. |
| **1830** | Bolívar dies. |
| **1847** | José Antonio Páez and his allies rule Venezuela as dictators. |
| **1854** | Slavery abolished. |
| **1888** | Dictator Antonio Guzmán Blanco establishes a stable, though corrupt, government in Venezuela. |
| **1914** | Oil well drilled on the shore of Lake Maracaibo. |
| **1935** | Dictator Juan Vincente Gómez rules Venezuela with violence, but remains in power because of a strong economy. |
| **1948** | Rómulo Gallegos, elected president by popular vote in 1947, takes office but is deposed by the military within the year. |
| **1952–1958** | General Marcos Pérez Jiménez rules as dictator. |
| **1954** | Hugo Rafael Chávez Frías is born in Sabaneta in the state of Barinas. |
| **1958** | The Democratic Action party (AD) and the Committee for Political Organization and Independent Election (COPEI) sign the pact of Punto Fijo, agreeing to share political power. |
| **1960** | Venezuela, Iraq, Iran, Kuwait, and Saudi Arabia form OPEC, the Organization of Petroleum Exporting Countries. |
| **1964** | Rómulo Betancourt serves as first popularly elected president of Venezuela. |

| 1975 | Hugo Chávez graduates from the Venezuelan Academy of Military Sciences. The government nationalizes the oil industry. |
|------|------|
| 1977 | Hugo Chávez marries Nancy Colmenares. |
| 1980 | Hugo Chávez returns to the military academy as an instructor. |
| 1982 | Hugo Chávez and other military officers form the Bolivarian Revolutionary Movement 200 (MBR-200). |
| 1988 | In a crumbling economy, former president Carlos Andrés Pérez is reelected to office. |
| 1989 | President Pérez implements neoliberal financial reforms, which lead to the *Caracazo*, the Caracan street riots. |
| 1992 | Hugo Chávez fails in an attempted *coup d'etat* of the Pérez government and is jailed. |
| 1993 | President Pérez is impeached for corruption. Rafael Caldera is elected president. |
| 1994 | President Caldera pardons Hugo Chávez and the other participants in the coup attempt. Chávez visits Cuba, divorces his wife, and organizes the revolutionary Fifth Republic Movement. |
| 1997 | Hugo Chávez marries Marisabel Rodríguez. |
| 1998 | Hugo Chávez is elected president of Venezeula by the largest majority of votes in the country's history. |
| 1999 | President Chávez launches Plan Bolivar 2000. Venezuela's new constitution is voted into effect. Landslides kill 15,000 to 20,000 people and leave 100,000 homeless. |
| 2000 | Hotly disputed elections create a new National Assembly and also reelect Hugo Chávez under the |

terms of the new constitution. Chávez visits Iraq and other OPEC members to strengthen OPEC's regulation of oil production and prices.

2001　Hugo Chávez enacts 49 decrees under the 2000 Enabling Act. Fedecámeras calls for general strike to oppose Chávez's policies.

2002　Attempted coup against Hugo Chávez fails. Chávez's wife, Marisabel Rodríguez, leaves him.

2002–2003　Business leaders and labor unions unite in two-month-long general strike, shutting down the oil industry and closing banks and schools.

2004　Recall referendum fails to unseat Hugo Chávez from office.

2005　*July.* Chávez government passes laws regulating media; new Venezuelan television station, *Telesur*, begins broadcasting.

*August.* U.S. Christian broadcaster Pat Robertson suggests that Chávez be assassinated to prevent Venezuela from becoming "a launching pad for communist infiltration and Muslim extremism."

*August.* Chávez offers soldiers, aid workers, food, and discounted oil to U.S. to help recovery from Hurricane Katrina.

*November.* Chávez provides discounted heating oil to residents of Massachusetts.

2006　*July.* Hugo Chávez and the Iranian president pledge mutual support.

*September.* Chávez calls U.S. President George W. Bush "the devil" at a United Nations speech.

# Bibliography

Anderson, Jon Lee. "The Revolutionary," *The New Yorker*, 9/10/01. http://www.newyorker.com/printables/archive/020422fr_archive03

Cannon, Barry. "Venezuela, April 2002: Coup or Popular Rebellion? The Myth of a United Venezuela." Bulletin of Latin American Research, 23:3, 2004, 285-302.

Chavez, Hugo and Marta Harnecker. *Understanding the Venezuelan Revolution: Hugo Chavez Hugo Talks to Marta Harnecker*. Translated by Chesa Boudin. New York: Monthly Review Press, 2005.

Ellison, Katharine. "Venezuela Steers a New Course." *The Smithsonian*. January 2006, pp. 60-71.

Encarnación, Omar G. "Venezuela's Civil Society Coup," *World Policy Journal*, Summer 2002, 38-48.

Guillermoprieto, Alma. "Don't Cry for Me, Venzuela," *The New York Review of Books*, 52:15, October 6, 2005.

Guevara, Aleida. *Chavez, Venezuela and the New Latin America*. New York: Ocean Press, 2005.

Gott, Richard. *Hugo Chavez and the Bolivarian Revolution*. New York: Verso, 2005.

Parenti, Christian. "Hugo Chavez and Petro Populism." The Nation, April 11, 2005. http://www.thenation.com/docprint.mhtml?i=20050411&s=parenti

Sontag, Deborah. "In the Time of Hugo Chavez." *New York Times Magazine,* June 2, 2002.

Wikipedia, The Free Encyclopedia. "Hugo Chavez." http://en.wikipedia.org/wiki/Hugo_Chavez

# FURTHER READING

Anderson, Jon Lee. "The Revolutionary." *New Yorker*, September 10, 2001.

Crooker, Richard A. *Venezuela*. New York: Chelsea House Publishers, 2006.

Fox, Geoffrey. *The Land and People of Venezuela*. New York: HarperCollins Publishers, 1991.

Guevara, Aleida. *Chávez, Venezuela and the New Latin America: An Interview with Hugo Chávez by Aleida Guevara*. New York: Ocean Press, 2005.

Winter, Jane Kohen. *Venezuela* (Cultures of the World Series). New York: Marshall Cavendish, 1998.

# PHOTO CREDITS

page:

3: Associated Press, GOVERNMENT

13: Associated Press, "THE 700 CLUB"

17: Associated Press, AP

20: Associated Press, AP

27: Getty Images

29: Getty Images

32: Getty Images

36: © CORBIS

42: © CORBIS

44: © Bettmann/CORBIS

47: © Pablo Corral V/CORBIS

52: © Bettmann/CORBIS

55: Associated Press, EL MERCURIO

62: © Michael Freeman/CORBIS

67: Associated Press, FILE

71: © Bill Gentile/ CORBIS

75: Associated Press, AP

78: Canadian Press, CP

82: Associated Press, AP

86: Associated Press, AP

92: Associated Press, AP

96: Associated Press, AP

100: Associated Press, AP

103: Associated Press, AP

107: Associated Press, AP

110: Associated Press, PRECIDENCIA

114: Associated Press, AP

115: Associated Press, MIRAFLORES PRESS

117: Associated Press, MIRAFLORES PRESS

Cover: © Juan Barreto/AFP/Getty Images

# INDEX

# ABOUT THE AUTHORS

**JUDITH LEVIN** is a writer living in New York City. She has published books for Rosen Publishing and Oxford University Press on subjects ranging from a biography of young adult author Christopher Paul Curtis to the history and excavation of the ancient Aztec city of Tenochtitlan.

**ARTHUR M. SCHLESINGER, JR.** is the leading American historian of our time. He won the Pulitzer Prize for his books *The Age of Jackson* (1945) and *A Thousand Days* (1965), which also won the National Book Award. Professor Schlesinger is the Albert Schweitzer Professor of the Humanities at the City University of New York and has been involved in several other Chelsea House projects, including the series *Revolutionary War Leaders*, *Colonial Leaders*, and *Your Government*.